Pay Less Tax!

...with help from Taxcafe's unique tax guides

All products available online at

www.taxcafe.co.uk

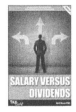

Popular Taxcafe titles include:

- *How to Save Property Tax*
- *Using a Property Company to Save Tax*
- *Tax-Free Capital Gains*
- *Salary versus Dividends*
- *Using a Company to Save Tax*
- *Small Business Tax Saving Tactics*
- *Keeping it Simple: Small Business Bookkeeping, Tax & VAT*
- *Non-Resident & Offshore Tax Planning*
- *How to Save Inheritance Tax*
- *Tax Saving Tactics for Salary Earners*
- *Pension Magic*
- *Isle of Man Tax Saving Guide*
- *How to Save Tax*

Taxcafe.co.uk Tax Guides

Tax-Free Capital Gains

How Non-Residents Can Protect Most
of their Property Profits from Tax

By Carl Bayley BSc ACA

Important Legal Notices:

Taxcafe®
TAX GUIDE – "Tax-Free Capital Gains"

Published by:
Taxcafe UK Limited
67 Milton Road
Kirkcaldy
KY1 1TL
United Kingdom
Tel: (01592) 560081

First Edition, June 2015

ISBN 978-1-907302-95-4

Disclaimer
Before reading or relying on the content of this Tax Guide, please read the
disclaimer.

Disclaimer

1. Please note that this publication is intended as **general guidance** only and does NOT constitute accountancy, tax, financial or other professional advice. The author and Taxcafe UK Limited make no representations or warranties with respect to the accuracy or completeness of the contents of this publication and cannot accept any responsibility for any liability, loss or risk, personal or otherwise, which may arise, directly or indirectly, from reliance on information contained in this publication.

2. Please note that tax legislation, the law and practices of government and regulatory authorities (e.g. HM Revenue and Customs) are constantly changing. Furthermore, your personal circumstances may vary from the general information contained in this tax guide which may not be suitable for your situation. We therefore recommend that for accountancy, tax, financial or other professional advice, you consult a suitably qualified accountant, tax specialist, independent financial adviser, or other professional adviser who will be able to provide specific advice based on your personal circumstances.

3. This guide covers UK taxation only and any references to 'tax' or 'taxation', unless the contrary is expressly stated, refer to UK taxation only. Please note that references to the 'UK' do not include the Channel Islands or the Isle of Man. Foreign tax implications are beyond the scope of this guide.

4. Whilst in an effort to be helpful this tax guide may refer to general guidance on matters other than UK taxation, Taxcafe UK Limited and the author are not expert in these matters and do not accept any responsibility or liability for loss which may arise from reliance on such information contained in this guide.

5. Please note that Taxcafe UK Limited has relied wholly on the expertise of the author in the preparation of the content of this tax guide. The author is not an employee of Taxcafe UK Limited but has been selected by Taxcafe UK Limited using reasonable care and skill.

About the Author

Carl Bayley is the author of a series of 'Plain English' tax guides designed specifically for the layman and the non-specialist. Carl's particular speciality is his ability to take the weird, complex and inexplicable world of taxation and set it out in the kind of clear, straightforward language that taxpayers themselves can understand. As he often says himself, "my job is to translate 'tax' into English".

Carl enjoys his role as a tax author, as he explains: "Writing these guides gives me the opportunity to use the skills and knowledge learned over almost thirty years in the tax profession for the benefit of a wider audience. The most satisfying part of my success as an author is the chance to give my readers the same standard of advice as the 'big guys' at a price which everyone can afford."

Carl takes the same approach when speaking on taxation, a role he frequently undertakes with great enthusiasm, including his highly acclaimed annual 'Budget Breakfast' for the Institute of Chartered Accountants.

In addition to being a recognised author and speaker on the subject, Carl has often spoken on taxation on radio and television, including the BBC's 'It's Your Money' programme and BBC Radio 2's Jeremy Vine Show.

Carl began his career as a Chartered Accountant in 1983 with one of the 'Big 4' accountancy firms. After qualifying as a double prize-winner, he immediately began specialising in taxation.

After honing his skills with several major international firms, Carl began the new millennium by launching his own tax and accounting practice, Bayley Miller Limited, through which he provides advice on a wide variety of taxation issues; especially property taxation and tax planning for small and medium-sized businesses.

Carl is a member of the governing Council of the Institute of Chartered Accountants in England and Wales, Chairman of the Institute's Tax Faculty, and a former President of ICAEW Scotland. He has co-organised the annual Peebles Tax Conference for the last 13 years.

When he isn't working, Carl takes on the equally taxing challenges of hill walking and creative writing – his Munro tally is now 82, but his first novel remains firmly in the planning stage!

Carl lives in Scotland with his partner Isabel and has four children.

Dedication

For the Past,

Firstly, I dedicate this book to the memory of those I have loved and lost:

First of all, to my beloved mother Diana – what would you think if you could see me now? The memory of your love warms me still. Thank you for making it all possible;

To my dear grandfather, Arthur - your wise words still come back to guide me; and to my loving grandmothers, Doris and Winifred;

Between you, you left me with nothing I could spend, but everything I need.

Also to my beloved friend and companion, Dawson, who waited so patiently for me to come home every night and who left me in the middle of our last walk together. Thank you for all those happy miles; I still miss you son.

For the Present,

Above all, I must dedicate this book to the person who stands, like a shining beacon, at the centre of every part of my life: Isabel, my 'life support system', whose unflinching support has seen me through the best and the worst. Whether anyone will ever call me a 'great man' I do not know, but I do know that I have a great woman behind me.

Without her help, support and encouragement, this book, and the others I have written, could never have been.

For the Future,

Finally, I also dedicate this book to four very special young people: Michelle – who is now very much a 'great woman' in her own right; Louise – the kind-hearted; James – the intellectual of the family; and Robert – the 'chip off the old block'.

I am so very proud of every one of you and I can only hope that I, in turn, will also be able to leave each of you with everything that you need.

Thanks

First and foremost, I must say an enormous thank you to Isabel: for all her help researching everything from obscure points of tax legislation to popular girls' names in Asia; for reading countless drafts; for making sure I stop to eat and sleep; and, most of all, for putting up with me when I'm under pressure. She is truly the other (and probably better) half of 'Carl Bayley'. I simply cannot ever thank her enough for everything that she does for me, but I intend to spend the rest of my life trying!

Thanks to the Taxcafe team, past and present, for their help in making these books far more successful than I could ever have dreamed.

I would like to thank my old friend and mentor, Peter Rayney, for his inspiration and for showing me that tax and humour can mix.

Thanks to Rebecca, Paul and David for taking me into the 'fold' at the Tax Faculty and for their fantastic support at our Peebles conference over many years.

And last, but far from least, thanks to Ann for keeping us right!

C.B., Roxburghshire, June 2015

Contents

Chapter 1 - Introduction   **1**
1.1   A Whole New World   1
1.2   The Ever-Expanding UK Tax Net   1
1.3   What Is Not Caught?   3
1.4   Scope Of This Guide   3
1.5   A Word About the Examples in This Guide   4
1.6   Some Terminology   4
1.7   UK Property Taxes   5
1.8   Double Taxation Agreements   6

Chapter 2 – Some UK Tax Basics   **8**
2.1   The UK Tax Year   8
2.2   Capital Gains Tax Rates   8
2.3   The Annual Exemption   10

Chapter 3 - What Gains Are Taxable on Non-Residents?   **11**
3.1   The Charge   11
3.2   Calculating the Taxable Gain   11
3.3   What Is Residential Property?   13
3.4   Excluded Property   14
3.5   Mixed Use   15
3.6   Changes of Use   17
3.7   Former Non-Residential Property   20
3.8   Temporary Disuse   22
3.9   Reporting Non-Resident Capital Gains   23
3.10   Paying Non-Resident Capital Gains Tax   23

Chapter 4 – Non-Residents with Current or Former   **24**
       Homes in the UK
4.1   What Happens if a UK Property is Used as the Owner's   24
       Home – Or Has Been in the Past?
4.2   Principal Private Residence Relief Basics   24
4.3   Private Letting Relief   26
4.4   Former Main Residences   26
4.5   Current Main Residences   28
4.6   Main Residence Elections   30
4.7   Non-Residents with Homes in the UK   32
4.8   Non-Residents with Current Homes in the UK   35
4.9   Meeting the '90 Day Test'   36
4.10   Recent Emigrants   39
4.11   Periods of Absence   41
4.12   Private Residences Held in Trust   45
4.13   Private Residences Held in Companies   45

Chapter 5 – Companies   46
5.1   Which Non-Resident Companies Are Caught?   46
5.2   Closely Held Company Rules   47
5.3   Closely Held Companies in Practice   48
5.4   Calculating the Charge   50
5.5   Enveloped Dwellings   52
5.6   The Annual Tax on Enveloped Dwellings & Related   54
        Charges

Chapter 6 – A Guide to Emigration and Residence   59
6.1   Introduction to Emigration   59
6.2   The Benefits of Emigration   59
6.3   Visits to the UK   62
6.4   Which Days Must Be Counted in a Visit?   67
6.5   The UK Home Test   67
6.6   Year of Death   68

Chapter 7 – Tax Saving Tips   69
7.1   Introduction   69
7.2   Existing Gains   69
7.3   Future Gains   70
7.4   Valuations   71
7.5   Change Your Portfolio   72
7.6   Using a Company   72
7.7   Furnished Holiday Lets   73
7.8   Further Considerations   74

Appendix A: UK Tax Rates and Allowances   75
         2014/15 to 2016/17

Appendix B: Retail Prices Index   76

Appendix C: The European Union &
         The European Economic Area   78

Chapter 1

Introduction

1.1 A WHOLE NEW WORLD

On 6th April 2015, the UK began taxing non-UK resident individuals and trusts, as well as many non-UK resident companies, on capital gains arising on the disposal of UK residential property.

This represents a major watershed in UK tax policy. Apart from the few exceptions discussed in Section 1.2, the UK has previously refrained from taxing non-UK residents on capital gains.

With this change, almost every person in the world who invests in UK residential property becomes exposed to UK Capital Gains Tax.

In short, the UK Treasury suddenly has a whole new world of people to tax!

In this guide, I will explore this new world and look at what it means for both current non-UK residents investing in UK property and UK resident investors planning to emigrate in future.

What we will see, as with many tax changes, is that whilst some of the potential savings have been diminished, there are still many opportunities to save tax by understanding the new regime and planning accordingly.

1.2 THE EVER-EXPANDING UK TAX NET

Non-UK residents have long been subject to tax on income from UK property but, prior to 6th April 2013, there were very few instances where a non-UK resident was subject to tax on a capital gain on UK property.

In fact, prior to that date, the only time a non-UK resident could suffer UK Capital Gains Tax was on the disposal of a property used in a trade carried on in the UK through a branch, agency or other permanent establishment. Such instances were rare and specifically excluded properties held purely as investments or to produce rental income. Even furnished holiday lets were excluded, despite their special status for many other tax purposes.

Then, from 6th April 2013, the UK began taxing companies and other 'non-natural' persons disposing of UK residential dwellings worth more than £2m which were held for (broadly speaking) the private use of the entity's owner or their family.

This charge, often referred to as 'ATED-related Capital Gains Tax' was expanded to cover property worth more than £1m from 6th April 2015 and will be further expanded to cover property worth more than £500,000 from 6th April 2016.

'ATED' stands for the Annual Tax on Enveloped Dwellings and this, together with the related Capital Gains Tax charge is covered in detail in Section 5.6. The interaction between 'ATED-related Capital Gains Tax' and other Capital Gains Tax charges on non-UK resident entities is also covered in Section 5.5.

Whilst 'ATED-related Capital Gains Tax' may potentially apply to any company or other 'non-natural' person holding UK residential property for private use, it is principally aimed at non-UK resident entities: which is why we have included it in this guide.

However, as important as 'ATED-related Capital Gains Tax' is for those who are affected by it, the main focus of this guide is the much more significant expansion in the scope of UK Capital Gains Tax from 6th April 2015. From that date onwards, any non-UK resident individual disposing of UK residential property may be subject to UK Capital Gains Tax.

Non-UK resident trusts disposing of UK residential property will also generally be subject to UK Capital Gains Tax from 6th April 2015 onwards, as well as many non-UK resident companies. We will take a closer look at the position for companies in Chapter 5.

In summary, we have moved quite rapidly from the position before 6th April 2013 where non-UK residents were very rarely subject to UK tax on UK property gains to the position from 6th April 2015 onwards where most non-UK residents will be subject to UK Capital Gains Tax on UK residential property (or on commercial property used in a trade carried on by the owner or their agent in the UK).

1.3 WHAT IS NOT CAUGHT?

Despite the ever-expanding UK tax net examined in the previous section, it is important to remember that UK Capital Gains Tax does not generally apply to the following types of property held by non-UK residents:

i)   Commercial property
ii) Overseas property

Commercial investment property held by non-UK residents generally remains exempt from UK Capital Gains Tax. However, as explained in Section 1.2, it is important to remember that property used in a trade carried on in the UK by the property's owner (or their agent) may be subject to UK Capital Gains Tax.

The UK cannot generally tax overseas property held by non-UK residents, although charges do sometimes apply where property is held by a non-UK resident entity owned by, or under the control of, UK resident individuals.

1.4 SCOPE OF THIS GUIDE

The purpose of this guide is to examine the UK Capital Gains Tax position for non-UK resident individuals, trusts and companies disposing of UK residential property. The guide is aimed at both those who are currently non-UK resident and those who intend to emigrate and thus become non-UK resident in future.

The only taxes covered in this guide are therefore UK Capital Gains Tax and the Annual Tax on Enveloped Dwellings (see Section 5.6).

Other UK taxes applying to non-UK residents investing in UK property are discussed briefly in Section 1.7 but are not covered in detail in this guide.

Foreign taxes are beyond the scope of this guide and are not covered herein. However, it is important to remember that non-UK residents investing in UK property will also generally be subject to tax in their country of residence. Each country has its own tax system, and income or gains which are exempt in the UK may nevertheless still be liable to tax elsewhere.

For tax purposes, the UK does not include the Channel Islands or the Isle of Man, but comprises only England, Scotland, Wales and Northern Ireland.

Finally, the reader must bear in mind the general nature of this guide. Individual circumstances vary and the tax implications of an individual's (or other entity's) actions will vary with them. For this reason, it is always vital to get professional advice before undertaking any tax planning or other transactions which may have tax implications. The author cannot accept any responsibility for any loss which may arise as a consequence of any action taken, or any decision to refrain from action taken, as a result of reading this guide.

1.5   A WORD ABOUT THE EXAMPLES IN THIS GUIDE

This guide is illustrated throughout by a number of examples.

In preparing the examples in this guide, I have assumed that the UK tax regime will remain unchanged in the future except to the extent of any Government announcements already made at the time of publication; including the Budget on 18th March 2015.

It is, however, important to understand that some Budget proposals are not yet law and may undergo some alteration before they are formally enacted.

Furthermore, if there is one thing which we can predict with any certainty, it is the fact that change **will** occur. The reader must bear this in mind when reviewing the results of our examples.

All persons described in the examples in this guide are entirely fictional characters created specifically for the purposes of this guide. Any similarities to actual persons, living or dead, or to fictional characters created by any other author, are entirely coincidental.

1.6   SOME TERMINOLOGY

In order to simplify matters slightly, the following terms will have the meanings described below throughout the rest of this guide:

Capital Gains Tax	UK Capital Gains Tax
Married couple	Legally married couple or members of a registered civil partnership
Non-resident	Not resident in the UK for tax purposes
Spouse partner	Legally married spouse or registered civil
Tax year	The UK tax year (see Section 2.1)

1.7   UK PROPERTY TAXES

As explained in Section 1.4, the primary focus of this guide is Capital Gains Tax payable by non-residents investing in UK property. The Annual Tax on Enveloped Dwellings is also covered, mostly in Chapter 5.

Other UK taxes which may affect non-residents investing in UK property include:

Income Tax
UK Income Tax is payable on rental profits derived from UK property by non-resident individuals, trusts or companies. This subject is covered in detail in the Taxcafe.co.uk guide *How to Save Property Tax*.

UK Income Tax may also be payable by non-resident individuals or trusts trading in UK property.

Corporation Tax
UK Corporation Tax may be payable by non-resident companies trading in UK property. Corporation Tax is covered in detail in the Taxcafe.co.uk guide *Using a Property Company to Save Tax*.

Stamp Duty Land Tax
From 1st April 2015, Stamp Duty Land Tax is payable on the purchase of property located in England, Wales or Northern Ireland. The tax generally ceased to apply to property in Scotland from that date. A higher rate of Stamp Duty Land Tax (15%) applies to property subject to the Annual Tax on Enveloped Dwellings (see Section 5.6).

Stamp Duty Land Tax is covered in detail in the Taxcafe.co.uk guides *How to Save Property Tax* and *Using a Property Company to Save Tax*.

Land and Buildings Transaction Tax

Land and Buildings Transaction Tax is payable on the purchase of property in Scotland after 31st March 2015. Land and Buildings Transaction Tax is covered in detail in the Taxcafe.co.uk guides *How to Save Property Tax* and *Using a Property Company to Save Tax*.

Inheritance Tax

Non-residents will generally remain subject to UK Inheritance Tax on UK property. Inheritance Tax is covered in detail in the Taxcafe.co.uk guide *How to Save Inheritance Tax*.

Council Tax

Council Tax is a local authority charge on the occupiers of UK residential property. Where a property is unoccupied, the charge will usually fall on the owner.

Business Rates

Business Rates (or 'Non-Domestic Rates') are a local authority charge on the occupiers of non-residential property in the UK. Where a property is unoccupied, the charge may fall on the owner.

Value Added Tax

Value Added Tax (or 'VAT' as it is commonly known in the UK) does not generally apply to UK residential property. It may, however, apply to commercial property in the UK. The subject of VAT on property is covered in detail in the Taxcafe.co.uk guides *How to Save Property Tax* and *Using a Property Company to Save Tax*.

1.8 DOUBLE TAXATION AGREEMENTS

All UK taxes payable by non-residents are subject to the terms of any applicable double taxation agreement between the non-resident's country of residence and the UK.

It is worth noting, however, that most double taxation agreements generally allow the country in which property is located to retain full taxing rights in respect of that property. Any double taxation relief due is generally given by way of some form of deduction or credit against the tax arising in the taxpayer's country of residence.

In other words, the UK will generally retain the right to tax income, gains or other transactions involving UK property according to UK domestic law and as set out in this guide.

For the purposes of this guide, I will therefore ignore the impact of any applicable double taxation agreement on the basis that there will seldom be any such impact in any case.

Readers should remember, however, that they will often have the right to claim a deduction or credit for any UK tax suffered against any tax liability arising in their country of residence on the same income, gain or other transaction.

I will refer to this right to claim a deduction for the UK tax suffered by a non-resident taxpayer in a few instances throughout this guide: where the taxpayer in one of my examples is resident in a suitable country.

However, it is important to remember that this right to a deduction will not always apply as it is dependent on the domestic law of the taxpayer's country of residence and the terms of any double taxation agreement between that country and the UK.

Readers should also take note of the 'wealth warning' at the end of Section 4.5.

Chapter 2

Some UK Tax Basics

2.1 THE UK TAX YEAR

For the purposes of both Income Tax and Capital Gains Tax, the UK tax year runs from 6th April in one calendar year to 5th April in the next.

Hence, for example, the UK tax year 2015/16 is the year ending 5th April 2016.

2.2 CAPITAL GAINS TAX RATES

Individuals generally pay Capital Gains Tax at two main rates:

- 18% on gains made by basic rate taxpayers
- 28% on gains made by higher rate taxpayers

The 'Higher Rate' of Capital Gains Tax

The higher rate of 28% applies to capital gains made by an individual to the extent that:

i) Their total taxable income for the tax year (after deducting their personal allowance and any other available deductions), plus

ii) Their total taxable capital gains arising during the tax year,

exceeds the Income Tax basic rate band (£31,785 for 2015/16).

In the case of a non-resident individual, their taxable income for these purposes will generally be their UK-source income only.

Many non-resident individuals are entitled to a personal allowance, including:

- British nationals resident abroad
- Nationals of other states within the European Economic Area (see Appendix C)
- Crown servants
- Residents of the Isle of Man
- Residents of the Channel Islands
- Residents of countries which have a suitable double taxation agreement with the UK

The personal allowance for 2015/16 is £10,600, meaning that non-resident individuals who are entitled to the allowance need to have total combined UK source income and taxable capital gains in the UK of £42,385 before they have to start paying Capital Gains Tax at 28%.

Those who are not entitled to a personal allowance only need to have total combined UK source income and taxable capital gains of £31,785 before they start paying Capital Gains Tax at 28%.

Non-resident individuals whose UK source income already exceeds these levels will pay Capital Gains Tax at 28% on all their taxable capital gains.

Those with lower levels of income will pay Capital Gains Tax at 18% on the first part of their capital gains until their basic rate band is exhausted. Thereafter, any further gains are taxed at 28%.

Example

Vladimir is resident in Russia for tax purposes and is not entitled to a personal allowance in the UK. In March 2016, he sells a UK residential property and realises a chargeable gain of £49,100.

Vladimir's total UK source income for 2015/16 is £19,785, meaning £12,000 of his basic rate band remains available (£31,785 - £19,785).

He deducts his annual exemption of £11,100 (see Section 2.3) from the £49,100 gain, leaving a taxable gain of £38,000. The first £12,000 is taxed at 18% and the remainder at 28%, giving him a tax bill of:

£12,000 x 18% =   £2,160
£26,000 x 28% =   £7,280
Total   £9,440

Entrepreneurs' Relief

A third, and more beneficial, rate of Capital Gains Tax (10%) applies where entrepreneurs' relief is available.

Sadly, however, entrepreneurs' relief is seldom available to property investors, except in the case of furnished holiday letting properties (see Section 7.7).

2.3 THE ANNUAL EXEMPTION

Each individual taxpayer is entitled to an annual exemption for every tax year. This includes **all** non-resident individuals subject to Capital Gains Tax. Unlike the Income Tax personal allowance, there are no additional qualifying requirements and the annual exemption is available to everyone.

Any unused annual exemption is simply lost; it cannot be carried forward.

The current annual exemption, for capital gains arising during the year ending 5th April 2016, is £11,100.

Chapter 3

What Gains Are Taxable on Non-Residents?

3.1 THE CHARGE

On 6th April 2015, the UK Government introduced a new Capital Gains Tax charge on non-residents disposing of UK residential property. The new charge will have a major impact on non-residents investing in UK property and on the planning issues facing UK resident investors intending to emigrate in the future.

The good news is that the new charge only applies to the part of the gain arising after 5th April 2015 (unless the taxpayer elects otherwise). Amongst other things, this means that emigration still remains a good tax planning strategy for those with significant capital gains arising before that date. We will take a more detailed look at the benefits of emigration in Chapter 6.

The non-resident Capital Gains Tax charge applies to non-resident individuals and trusts, as well as some non-resident companies. Individuals will pay Capital Gains Tax at normal rates (as set out in Section 2.2) and will be entitled to the annual exemption (see Section 2.3). As with other gains, trusts will pay Capital Gains Tax at 28% and be entitled to a reduced annual exemption. The position for companies is examined in Chapter 5.

3.2 CALCULATING THE TAXABLE GAIN

The amount of gain subject to the new charge will generally be limited to the increase in the property's value from 5th April 2015 to the date of sale. The main, 'default' method for calculating this increase is to base it on the property's market value at 5th April 2015, although taxpayers may alternatively elect to either:

a)   Use a straight line apportionment method, or
b)   Be subject to tax on the gain over their entire period of ownership

As we shall see in the examples that follow, the straight line apportionment method will produce savings in many cases.

Example

Barack is US resident for tax purposes. On 5th April 2009, he bought a house in London for £500,000. The property was worth £675,000 on 5thApril 2015 and he sells it for £710,000 on 5th April 2016.

Under the main, 'default' method, Barack would be subject to Capital Gains Tax on a gain of £35,000 (£710,000 - £675,000).

In this case, however, Barack should elect to use the straight line apportionment method. His overall gain is £210,000 (£710,000 - £500,000), but he is only subject to Capital Gains Tax for one year out of a total ownership period of seven years, so this method would give him a chargeable gain of just £30,000 (£210,000 x 1/7).

Whichever method Barack uses, he will be entitled to the 2015/16 annual exemption of £11,100. Assuming he makes the straight line apportionment election and has no other chargeable gains in the UK in 2015/16, this will leave him with a taxable gain of £18,900 (£30,000 – £11,100).

If we also assume that Barack has little or no UK-source income in the same 2015/16 tax year then his basic rate band will be available to ensure that he only has to pay Capital Gains Tax at just 18% (see Section 2.2).

Barack's Capital Gains Tax bill, at 18%, will thus be £3,402 (£18,900 x 18%). He should be able to claim relief for this against any US tax liability he has on the sale.

The Entire Period of Ownership Method

The option to be taxed on the gain arising over the owner's entire period of ownership will seldom be beneficial: it would certainly not have been appropriate in Barack's case as he would have then had a chargeable gain of £210,000 instead of just £30,000!

This option may, however, be beneficial in a few cases where a property has undergone a 'change of use'. This concept is examined in Section 3.6 and an example of when an election to be taxed on the gain over the entire period of ownership might be beneficial is given in Section 3.7.

3.3   WHAT IS RESIDENTIAL PROPERTY?

The non-resident Capital Gains Tax charge applies to UK residential property only.

Most forms of legal or equitable interest in UK residential property are caught. This obviously includes freehold or leasehold interests, but would generally also include any other form of title or interest on which a capital gain might arise.

In particular, a contract for an off-plan purchase of property which is to be constructed or adapted for use as residential property is caught.

Residential property is defined as any interest in UK property which includes one or more dwellings.

For these purposes, a property, or a part of a property, is a dwelling at any time when it is:

- In use as a dwelling
- Suitable for use as a dwelling
- In the process of being constructed or adapted for use as a dwelling

The term 'dwelling' is not specifically defined in the new legislation but guidance and case law relating to other areas of UK tax legislation suggest that a dwelling is a building, or a part of a building, which contains 'the facilities required for day-to-day private domestic existence'. We will take a closer look at what this means in practice in Section 3.5.

The new legislation does specify that a dwelling includes the gardens or grounds, and any outbuildings, which belong with it.

Hence, in the simple case of a single, stand-alone house, the entire property, including any garden, grounds or outbuildings, is a single dwelling and is all subject to the new tax charge.

Wealth Warning

It is important to understand that **any** non-resident disposing of **any** UK property (after 5th April 2015) which includes one or more dwellings (as defined above) at **any** time during their 'relevant ownership period' must report that disposal to HM Revenue and Customs.

We will take a closer look at these reporting requirements in Section 3.9.

The 'relevant ownership period' for this purpose means the period beginning on the later of:

- The date of purchase of the property, and
- 6th April 2015

and ending on the day before the date of disposal of the property.

3.4   EXCLUDED PROPERTY

A number of types of property which include overnight accommodation are specifically excluded from the new charge, including:

- School dormitories (residential accommodation for school pupils)
- Barracks (residential accommodation for members of the armed forces)
- Children's homes
- Residential care homes (for the elderly, disabled, mentally ill or those suffering from dependence on drugs or alcohol)
- Hospitals and hospices
- Prisons
- Hotels and inns
- Other residential institutions (e.g. monasteries)
- Student halls of residence

Under the last category, a property is also excluded if it has 15 or more bedrooms, was purpose built for students and is occupied by students on more than half of the days in the year.

If a non-resident owned a guest house, which they also use as their home, or which is used as a home by a close relative or other associate of the owner, then this would amount to 'mixed use': a concept which we will examine in Section 3.5.

3.5   MIXED USE

Where a property has mixed use (i.e. simultaneous residential and non-residential use) gains should be apportioned on a 'just and reasonable' basis with the residential element being chargeable to Capital Gains Tax.

Example

Tony is a non-resident but owns a guest house in Scotland which is occupied and run by his son Gordon. Gordon uses 30% of the property as his home and the remaining 70% is occupied and used by guests.

The property is worth £200,000 on 5th April 2015 and Tony sells it a few years later for £300,000.

The gain arising after 5th April 2015 is therefore £100,000 but Tony is only subject to Capital Gains Tax on the residential portion of the gain: £30,000 (£100,000 x 30%).

In this example, I have taken the simplistic view that 70% of the property is in business use.

In practice, arriving at a 'just and reasonable' apportionment is a much more complex matter and there are many ways of approaching it, such as:

- Professional valuations
- Number of rooms
- Floor area

Let's look at another example to see how we might arrive at a 'just and reasonable' apportionment in practice.

Example

Sam owns a large house, part of which is used as a dance studio. The studio operates on a commercial basis, so this part of the property can be regarded as being in business use.

The house has a total of ten rooms, excluding kitchens, bathrooms and hallways. The studio (one room) is mostly used for business but it is also used privately about 10% of the time. There is also a reception/office area adjacent to the studio and this room is only ever used for business.

Sam therefore has a ten room property with one room in exclusive business use and one room used 90% for business. It would therefore be 'just and reasonable' to say that her property has 19% business use and 81% residential use.

However, Sam feels that this apportionment is not entirely fair because the studio is a very large room compared with the other rooms in the house. In fact, the studio has a floor area of 150 square metres – a large proportion of her house's total floor area of 500 square metres. The reception/office area measures 12 square metres and there is also a bathroom measuring 8 square metres which is used by the studio customers around 75% of the time.

Sam can therefore calculate her house's business use as follows:

Studio – 150 x 90%   *135*
Reception/office – 12 x 100%   *12*
Bathroom – 8 x 75%   *6*
Total: *153*

This total of 153 amounts to 30.6% as a proportion of the house's total floor area of 500 square metres. Hence, it would be 'just and reasonable' for Sam to claim 30.6% business use of her property, making her (as a non-resident) taxable on just 69.4% of the gain arising after 5th April 2015.

As we can see from this example, different methods of arriving at a 'just and reasonable' apportionment can produce very different results. It is often worth looking at different methods to see which works best for you but the important watchword to always remember (and the clue is in the 'title') is to be reasonable.

Examples of Mixed Use

Common examples of mixed use include:

- Guest houses
- Properties occupied and used by professionals as both a home and a business e.g. doctors, dentists, vets, dance teachers, etc.
- Buildings which incorporate shops or offices at ground level with residential flats above them

Another interesting example is a property divided into self-contained flats. Each of the flats contains 'the facilities required for day-to-day private domestic existence' and is therefore a dwelling; so these parts of the property are treated as residential.

But existing guidance and practice in other areas of tax law suggest that the communal areas within the property (hallways, stairs, shared facilities such as utility rooms, etc.) are not part of a dwelling and hence not in residential use for the purposes of the Capital Gains Tax charge on a non-resident owner disposing of the property.

The logical conclusion of this line of thought is that a property divided into self-contained flats is therefore in mixed use and part of the gain arising is not subject to Capital Gains Tax where the owner is non-resident.

It is too soon to know whether such an argument will succeed in practice but it is certainly valid in theory.

3.6 CHANGES OF USE

In most cases, property remains in either residential use or non-residential use throughout its life; or at least throughout a person's ownership.

In some cases, however, a property, or part of a property, will undergo a change of use: either from residential to non-residential, or vice versa.

In such cases, the gain is apportioned to reflect the number of days of residential use out of the total period of ownership which is subject to Capital Gains Tax.

But when exactly is the residential use deemed to begin, or end?

As we know from Section 3.3, a property, or part of a property, becomes a 'dwelling' as soon as any work begins to construct or adapt it for residential use.

A property ceases to be a dwelling at the commencement of any 'works' as a result of which the property will either cease to exist or become unsuitable for use as a dwelling. However, this period can only be excluded from the Capital Gains Tax charge if the following conditions are met by the date of disposal of the property:

- The property has ceased to exist or become unsuitable for use as a dwelling as a result of the works
- Planning permission and/or change of use consent, as appropriate, has been granted
- The works have been carried out in accordance with such permission and/or consent

For the purpose of the above conditions, the date of disposal is the date of completion. This differs from the basic Capital Gains Tax rule that the date of disposal is usually the date of contract (or the date that a contract becomes unconditional).

If the works commence before planning permission or change of use consent has been granted then the property is deemed to remain in residential use until the date that permission or consent is granted.

Furthermore, if there is any time at which works are being carried out which are not in accordance with the relevant planning permission or consent then that period is also deemed to be a period of residential use.

Example

Juan is resident in Spain for tax purposes but owns a large house in Devon which he purchased for £250,000 on 5th April 2005. On 5th April 2015 the house was worth £350,000.

In 2017 Juan decides to convert the house into a hotel. The conversion work starts in June that year, but the relevant planning permission and change of use consent is only granted on 5th October 2017.

The cost of the conversion work amounts to £75,000 and the property is then run as a hotel until Juan sells it for £650,000 on 5th April 2020.

The first point to note is, although Juan has sold a commercial property (a hotel), he must report this disposal to HM Revenue and Customs because the property was in residential use during his 'relevant ownership period' (see Section 3.3).

The total gain arising during Juan's relevant ownership period is £225,000. This is his sale proceeds of £650,000 less the property's market value at 5th April 2015, £350,000, less the conversion costs of £75,000. (Note that all of the conversion costs are deductible, even though some of the work was carried out before planning permission and change of use consent were granted.)

The property was deemed to cease to be in residential use on 5th October 2017: the date that planning permission and change of use consent were granted. Hence, only two and a half years (5th April 2015 to 5th October 2017) out of the total relevant ownership period of five years (5th April 2015 to 5th April 2020) are chargeable to Capital Gains Tax.

Juan's chargeable gain is thus £112,500 (£225,000 x 2.5/5).

Similar principles apply if Juan elects for straight-line apportionment on his gain (see Section 3.2).

His total gain over his entire ownership period from 2005 to 2020 is £325,000 (sale proceeds, £650,000, less cost, £250,000, less conversion costs, £75,000). Firstly, this is time apportioned to arrive at the post-5th April 2015 element, £108,333 (£325,000 x 5/15). This is then apportioned again to derive the residential element. As before, we multiply the gain by a factor of 2.5/5 to arrive at a chargeable gain of £54,167. Clearly this is Juan's better option in this case.

A property may also be deemed to have ceased to be in residential use during a period when the property is unoccupied and which is:

- Immediately prior to the commencement of works which themselves qualify as set out above, and
- A period when the property is not being used as a dwelling for reasons which are connected with those works

When Does A Property Cease to Exist?

A property ceases to exist when it is either demolished to ground level or demolished to ground level except for one or two facades which have been retained as a condition of planning permission.

3.7 FORMER NON-RESIDENTIAL PROPERTY

In Section 3.6 we looked at an example of a residential property being changed into a non-residential property.

Let's now look at an example of the opposite situation: a non-residential property being changed into a residential property.

Example

On 5th October 1996 Silvio bought a shop in Kent for £75,000. The property was worth £400,000 on 5th April 2015.

The property was run as a shop until 5th October 2016 when work began to convert it into a residential flat. The conversion work cost £40,000, and the converted property was rented out for about a year until Silvio sold it for £600,000 on 5th April 2018.

Silvio is a non-resident for tax purposes so he is only subject to Capital Gains Tax on the residential portion of his gain. As we know from Section 3.2, he has three options for calculating his chargeable gain.

The 'Default' Method
Under the default method, Silvio's total gain during the relevant ownership period (see Section 3.3) would be £160,000 (sale proceeds, £600,000, less value at 5th April 2015, £400,000, less conversion costs, £40,000).

The property was deemed to be in residential use for eighteen months (October 2016 to April 2018) out of a relevant ownership period of three years, or 36 months (April 2015 to April 2018). Hence, Silvio's chargeable gain under the default method would be £80,000 (£160,000 x 18/36).

Straight Line Apportionment

Using straight line apportionment, we first calculate the gain arising over Silvio's entire period of ownership. This amounts to £485,000 (sale proceeds, £600,000, less cost, £75,000, less conversion costs, £40,000).

His total period of ownership was 21.5 years, so the time apportioned gain for the relevant ownership period of three years is £67,674 (£485,000 x 3/21.5).

This is time apportioned once more to arrive at the chargeable gain relating to the eighteen month period of residential use: £33,837 (£67,674 x 18/36).

The Entire Period of Ownership Method

As we know, the gain arising over Silvio's entire period of ownership is £485,000.

If, as a non-resident, he elects to be taxed over his entire period of ownership, he will be exempt on the first 20 years of his ownership period when the property was being used as a shop. He will only be chargeable to Capital Gains Tax on the last eighteen months (1.5 years) of residential use.

His chargeable gain will thus be £33,837 (£485,000 x 1.5/21.5).

As we can see, in this case, both of the alternative methods for calculating Silvio's chargeable gain produce a better result than the main 'default' method. In fact, they both produce the same result: which is logical because they both tax an eighteen month period out of a total ownership period of 21.5 years.

For an individual, both of these alternative methods will always be available but, as explained in Section 5.5, for companies and other corporate entities, it may be necessary to use the entire period of ownership method.

3.8 TEMPORARY DISUSE

Simply not using a property is not sufficient to get you 'off the hook' since, as we saw in Section 3.3, a property is deemed to be a dwelling at any time when it is suitable for use as a dwelling.

A property might, however, become temporarily unsuitable for use as a dwelling.

Sadly, the general rule is that temporary unsuitability is generally disregarded unless:

- It arises due to damage
- The damage was accidental or beyond the control of the owner
- The property was unsuitable for use as a dwelling for at least 90 days as a result of the damage
- The period of unsuitability ends during the owner's ownership period

The damage must not have been caused during alteration works which were already expected to have made the building unsuitable for use as a dwelling for at least 30 days in any case.

Example

Hilary is a US resident with a house in Norfolk which was worth £500,000 on 5th April 2015. (The house that is; Norfolk is probably worth more than that!)

On 20th September 2015, an exceptionally high tide causes severe flood damage to Hilary's house and it becomes unusable. The necessary repair work takes several months and is only completed on 20th March 2016.

Hilary gets a new job in January 2017 and no longer has enough spare time for visiting her holiday home in Norfolk, so she sells it for £700,000 on 5th April 2017.

Hilary's total gain over her relevant ownership period is £200,000 but she is able to exclude the six month period during which the flood damage was being repaired. This means that only 18 months out of her relevant ownership period of 24 months are chargeable, so her chargeable gain is £150,000 (£200,000 x 18/24).

Note that Hilary cannot claim any Capital Gains Tax deduction for the cost of repair work on her holiday home. She could, however, claim any part of the cost which related to improvements. For further details on the distinction between repairs and improvements see the Taxcafe.co.uk guide *How to Save Property Tax*.

3.9 REPORTING NON-RESIDENT CAPITAL GAINS

Non-residents disposing of UK residential property after 5th April 2015 are required to report their disposal to HM Revenue and Customs within 30 days.

As explained in the 'wealth warning' in Section 3.3, this includes any disposal of any property which has been wholly or partly in residential use at any time during the relevant ownership period (i.e. since the later of 6th April 2015 or the date of purchase).

Severe penalties apply for failure to report a disposal within the required time limit: even when no tax is actually due!

Non-residents who are in the UK Income Tax self-assessment system will also need to report their chargeable gains through that system

3.10 PAYING NON-RESIDENT CAPITAL GAINS TAX

Non-residents who are already in the UK Income Tax self-assessment system can pay any Capital Gains Tax due by the normal date: 31st January following the relevant UK tax year.

Taxpayers who are not in the self-assessment system must pay any Capital Gains Tax due within 30 days of the relevant property disposal.

Chapter 4

Non-Residents with Current or Former Homes in the UK

4.1 WHAT HAPPENS IF A UK PROPERTY IS USED AS THE OWNER'S HOME – OR HAS BEEN IN THE PAST?

Where a property has been used as an individual's main residence (i.e. their principal home) at any time during their period of ownership, that individual owner is entitled to an important Capital Gains Tax relief known as 'principal private residence relief'.

Furthermore, it is sometimes possible for a non-resident individual with a home in the UK to elect for their UK home to be treated as their main residence for UK Capital Gains Tax purposes. This procedure is examined in Section 4.6.

There are therefore two types of non-resident individual who may be able to benefit from principal private residence relief:

- Those with a former main residence in the UK
- Non-residents with a home in the UK

As we shall see in the sections that follow, where main residence status can be established for a property at **any time** during the owner's period of ownership, principal private residence relief can be extremely powerful and can reduce the amount of Capital Gains Tax payable on a disposal quite significantly.

4.2 PRINCIPAL PRIVATE RESIDENCE RELIEF BASICS

Principal private residence relief exempts the gain, or part of the gain, on a property which has been the owner's only or main residence for some or all of their ownership period.

Prior to 6th April 2015, this relief was of no importance to non-residents since they were not generally subject to Capital Gains Tax in any case.

Now the relief may be hugely important to non-residents since it may be possible to claim an exemption for part of the gain arising on UK residential property which has been used as their main residence at some time during their ownership.

Furthermore, as we shall see in Section 4.6, some non-residents with homes in the UK may be able to obtain the same relief on their UK home by making a suitable election.

Principal private residence relief operates on a time apportionment basis and exempts:

i) The portion of the ownership period during which the property was the owner's main residence,
ii) Any part of the last eighteen months of the ownership period which is not already included under (i),
iii) Certain periods of temporary absence from the property (see Section 4.11), and
iv) Up to twelve months at the beginning of the ownership period when the property is being prepared for occupation as the owner's main residence, or during which the owner is unable to sell their previous main residence

Subject to some very rare exceptions, only one property can qualify as the owner's main residence at any given time. In other words, the period under (i) above can generally only apply to one property at any given time.

For a non-resident, these periods of exemption will generally only be of any benefit where they fall after 5th April 2015: since principal private residence relief can only be claimed on the part of the gain which is actually taxable.

Nonetheless, at the very least, even former homes occupied as a main residence before April 2015 will benefit from the final eighteen months period under (ii) above. We will look at this simple scenario in Section 4.4.

Far greater savings will be available in other cases!

Married Couples

For the purposes of principal private residence relief, a legally married couple, or a couple in a registered civil partnership, can only have one main residence between them at any given time.

More Information on Principal Private Residence Relief

In this section, I have given you a brief introduction to principal private residence relief. A great deal more information on the relief can be found in the Taxcafe.co.uk guide *How to Save Property Tax*.

4.3 PRIVATE LETTING RELIEF

Where a property qualifies for principal private residence relief, but has also been rented out as residential accommodation by the owner at some time during their period of ownership, it also qualifies for a further relief, known as private letting relief. Private letting relief is the lowest of the following three amounts:

- i) The amount of principal private residence relief available on the property
- ii) The amount of gain arising due to the letting
- iii) £40,000 (per person)

In the case of a non-resident, only periods of letting falling after 5th April 2015 can be counted for this purpose.

Note that the £40,000 limit operates on a 'per person' basis. A couple owning property jointly might therefore be able to claim up to £80,000 of relief.

We will see several examples of private letting relief in operation later in this chapter.

4.4 FORMER MAIN RESIDENCES

As a simple introduction to how principal private residence relief operates in practice, let's look at the basic position for a non-resident individual disposing of a former main residence in the UK.

Example

Angela lived in the UK for many years before returning to Germany in 2013, where she is now resident for tax purposes. On 5th April 1999, Angela purchased a house in Cheltenham for £160,000 and used it as her main residence until 5th April 2009. She then rented the property out until 5th April 2013, when she adopted it as a holiday home for use during her return visits to the UK.

The house was worth £460,000 on 5th April 2015. Four years later, on 5th April 2019, Angela sells it for £640,000.

As a non-resident, Angela will be subject to Capital Gains Tax on the gain of £180,000 (£640,000 - £460,000) arising over the 48 month period from April 2015 to April 2019. However, as the property was her main residence in the past, she is able to claim exemption for her last 18 months of ownership. The exemption amounts to £67,500 (£180,000 x 18/48). She is not entitled to claim private letting relief, as she did not rent the property out during the period for which she is chargeable to Capital Gains Tax (i.e. the period from 6th April 2015 to the date of sale).

Under the 'default' method for calculating her gain, Angela therefore has a chargeable gain of £112,500 (£180,000 - £67,500).

Angela can also choose from two other alternative methods for calculating her gain:

Under the straight line apportionment method, the gain would be £96,000 (£640,000 - £160,000 = £480,000 x 4/20). Angela could then deduct principal private residence relief of £36,000 (£96,000 x 18/48), leaving her with a chargeable gain of £60,000.

By electing to tax the £480,000 gain arising over her whole period of ownership, Angela would be entitled to principal private residence relief for the ten years that she lived in the property and her last 18 months of ownership: a total of 11.5 years, or £276,000 (£480,000 x 11.5/20). Under this option, she would also be entitled to private letting relief: as her rental period is now being taken into account in her gain calculation. However, the relief would be limited to £40,000, leaving her with a chargeable gain of £164,000 (£480,000 - £276,000 - £40,000).

Clearly, Angela's best option is to elect for the straight line apportionment method!

Once again, this example also demonstrates that the entire period of ownership method will seldom be of any benefit. I included it here simply to make that point.

Whichever method Angela uses to calculate her chargeable gain, she will be entitled to claim the 2018/19 annual exemption (unless she uses it against any other chargeable gains in the UK for that year). Her UK tax may also be deducted against any German tax liability which she has on the property sale.

4.5   CURRENT MAIN RESIDENCES

Another important scenario to consider is a future sale of a current main residence. In other words, the position on the main home of an individual who is currently UK resident, but who emigrates and becomes non-resident before eventually selling their current home at a later date.

Example

Julia and Kevin own a house in South London which was worth £800,000 on 5th April 2015. It has been their main residence for several years and remains so until they emigrate to Australia on 5th April 2017.

They rent the house out for a few years, until they eventually sell it for £1.2m on 5th April 2023 whilst still resident in Australia.

The gain arising over their relevant ownership period of eight years (2015 to 2023) is £400,000 (£1.2m - £800,000).

The couple are entitled to principal private residence relief for the part of this period that the property was their main residence (April 2015 to April 2017) and for their last eighteen months of ownership. This totals 3.5 years, so their principal private residence relief amounts to £175,000 (£400,000 x 3.5/8).

As the couple rented the property out during their relevant ownership period, they may also claim private letting relief. This is limited to £40,000 each, or £80,000 in total.

The couple therefore have a total chargeable gain of £145,000 (£400,000 - £175,000 - £80,000), or £72,500 each.

If the couple have no other chargeable gains in the UK in 2022/23, they will each be able to deduct their annual exemption. If we estimate this as £12,500 then Julia and Kevin will each have a taxable capital gain of £60,000. As explained in Section 2.2, the rate of tax applying to these gains will depend on the level of Julia and Kevin's UK source income for 2022/23.

As usual, it will be worthwhile for Julia and Kevin to consider whether an election for straight line apportionment might be worthwhile.

Example Continued

Let us suppose that Julia and Kevin brought their property for £450,000 on 5th April 2011. The total gain arising over their entire period of ownership of 12 years is therefore £750,000 (£1.2m - £450,000).

*The time apportioned gain for the relevant ownership of eight years is thus £500,000 (£750,000 x 8/12). This is greater than the gain derived under the default method, so the election to use straight line apportionment is **not** beneficial in this case.*

Julia and Kevin should not elect for straight line apportionment of their gain in this case. For the **sake of illustration only**, however, let's look at what would happen if they did make the election:

Example Part 3

As before, Julia and Kevin would be entitled to principal private residence relief for 3.5 years out of their relevant ownership period of eight years. This would now amount to £218,750 (£500,000 x 3.5/8). They would also be entitled to private letting relief of £40,000 each, as before. The couple's total chargeable gain would thus now be £201,250 (£500,000 - £218,750 - £80,000), or £100,625 each.

Deducting their estimated annual exemptions of £12,500 each would leave Julia and Kevin with taxable gains of £88,125 each: £28,125 more than under the default method.

Using straight line apportionment would be a costly mistake in this case. The couple would end up paying an additional £7,875 each in Capital Gains Tax (£28,125 x 28%) – a total extra unnecessary cost of £15,750.

Wealth Warning

There are two reasons why a couple like Julia and Kevin might elect for straight line apportionment in a case like this:

- To avoid the need to have their property valued at 5th April 2015
- Because they believe that the extra tax paid in the UK would be deductible against the tax arising in their country of residence anyway, leaving them no worse off

However, many country's own tax systems will only provide double tax relief for the minimum amount which would have been payable in the country where the tax arises if all applicable reliefs, exemptions, claims, etc were made. In other words, a couple like Julia and Kevin might be denied any relief in their own country for the additional extra unnecessary tax paid in the UK.

4.6 MAIN RESIDENCE ELECTIONS

Where an individual, or a married couple, has more than one private residence, they may elect which of these is to be treated as their main residence for Capital Gains Tax purposes.

It follows that a property cannot be the owner's main residence unless it is a private residence of the owner or their spouse.

Note that, for this purpose, a person is only your spouse so long as you continue to live together as a couple and are not separated under a court order or under circumstances which are likely to become permanent.

The concept of when a property may be your private residence is examined in detail in the Taxcafe guide *How to Save Property Tax* but, in essence, you will generally need to be using the property as a home.

At one stage, it was feared that the ability to make main residence elections would be withdrawn after 5th April 2015 in order to prevent someone like Angela (in our example in Section 4.4) from simply electing to treat her UK property as her main residence for UK tax purposes and thus avoiding any Capital Gains Tax when she sold it.

Thankfully, the Government has adopted a slightly different approach. The ability to make main residence elections has been retained but a new rule has been introduced which stipulates that, for Capital Gains Tax purposes, a property cannot be the owner's private residence for any tax year unless the owner is either:

 a) Resident for tax purposes (for at least half of that tax year) in the country in which the property is located, or
b) Physically present in the property at midnight on at least 90 days during that tax year

For the second test, 'days' spent in the property by the owner's spouse may also be counted, as well as 'days' spent (by either of them) in another residential property which the taxpayer owns in the same country (but the same 'day' cannot be counted twice).

For the years in which the property is purchased or sold, the 90 day requirement is proportionately reduced, as appropriate. For example, where a property was purchased on 1st May 2015, the test under (b) above becomes 84 days (90 x 340/366 – rounded up).

With some very careful planning, some non-residents with homes in the UK will be able to maintain their non-resident status and yet still be able to nominate their UK home as their main residence for Capital Gains Tax purposes: thus avoiding the new charge. We will look at some of the potential benefits of this in Sections 4.9 and 4.10.

To achieve this feat, however, it will be essential to bear in mind the statutory residence rules set out in Chapter 6 and, in particular, the 'UK Home Test' set out in Section 6.5.

A close look at these rules will reveal that this will be extremely difficult for any unmarried individual who has only recently emigrated!

Time Limits for Main Residence Elections

The general rule is that a main residence election must be made within two years of the date on which an individual, or a married couple, first has a new combination of two or more private residences.

However, since non-residents cannot have been expected to know that they would need to do a main residence election, they are permitted to make a retrospective election, covering any periods which qualify under the above rules, when they come to sell their UK property.

This will automatically vary any previous elections in respect of another property, provided that the other property has not yet been sold. Naturally, a retrospective election cannot be made in respect of a period for which principal private residence relief has already been claimed on another property.

Married Couples

Married couples who each have an interest in one or more private residences must make a joint main residence election.

4.7   NON-RESIDENTS WITH HOMES IN THE UK

As we have seen in Section 4.6, some non-residents with homes in the UK may be able to make a main residence election in favour of their UK property. In the next few sections, we will look at when this might be possible and just how beneficial it could be.

Firstly, it is worth bearing in mind that a retrospective election may be made at the time of the disposal of the property. This election can cover any qualifying period (under the rules set out in Section 4.6) for which principal private residence relief has not been claimed on any other property.

The types of non-resident who are most likely to be able to benefit from main residence elections are:

- Married couples,
- Individuals who have never been UK resident,
- Individuals who have been non-resident for a long time, and
- Individuals who maintained homes in the UK prior to 6th April 2013 (when the statutory residence test set out in Chapter 6 was introduced)

Example

Benito and Rachele have never been UK resident, but have kept a holiday home on the Isle of Wight since 5th June 1989, when they bought it for £60,000.

In the years from 1989 to 2012, the couple spent most summers in the property but were able to maintain non-resident status under the rules then applying.

In 2013, the couple began renting the property out. It was worth £600,000 on 5th April 2015 and they eventually sold it for £780,000 on 5th June 2019.

Under the main 'default' method, the gain arising during the couple's relevant ownership period of 50 months is £180,000 (£780,000 - £600,000).

Under the straight line apportionment method, the gain of £720,000 (£780,000 - £60,000) arising over their total ownership period of 360 months is apportioned, leaving a chargeable gain for the period after 5th April 2015 of £100,000 (£720,000 x 50/360). The couple therefore elect to use this method.

Having checked their diaries, the couple realise that they are entitled to make a main residence election in favour of the property for the 2012/13 tax year. They make the election and this then entitles them to principal private residence relief for their last 18 months of ownership. This amounts to £36,000 (£100,000 x 18/50).

As they have rented the property out during their relevant ownership period, they are also entitled to private letting relief of £36,000.

The total chargeable gain is thus reduced to £28,000 (£100,000 - £36,000 - £36,000), or £14,000 each. If we estimate the 2019/20 annual exemption at £12,000, and assume that neither of them have any other chargeable gains in the UK that year, this will leave them with a taxable gain of just £2,000 each.

Depending on the level of their UK income for 2019/20, Benito and Rachele would each have a Capital Gains Tax bill of between £360 (18%) and £560 (28%) – a total of between £720 and £1,120.

Without the main residence election, the couple would have each had a taxable gain of £38,000 (£100,000/2 - £12,000), giving them Capital Gains Tax bills of up to £10,640 each, or £21,280 in total.

The election may therefore save the couple over £20,000! (Up to £20,160 to be precise: £21,280 - £1,120)

Tax Tip

A main residence election in favour of a UK property for any period prior to 6th April 2015 will have the same effect for a non-resident: no matter how short the period of main residence is.

Any non-resident with more than one UK home prior to that date should keep the pre-6th April 2015 period covered by the election as short as possible, as this will leave other periods available for possible elections in favour of other properties.

Example

Wilhelm had two homes in the UK prior to April 2015, one in London and one in Wales. They have both been rental properties since then. Wilhelm spent more than 90 days in his London home in 2009/10. He acquired his home in Wales in May 2010. He spent more than 90 days in total in both properties in 2011/12.

When Wilhelm sells his London home, he should make a main residence election covering only the 2009/10 tax year. In this way, he will also later be able to make a main residence election in favour of his Welsh home (covering the 2011/12 tax year).

4.8 NON-RESIDENTS WITH CURRENT HOMES IN THE UK

In the previous section we saw the benefits of a main residence election in favour of a property which was used as a UK home by a non-resident in the past.

We now turn to planning how to obtain a period of qualifying main residence for a current UK home.

There are two ways of doing this:

- Become UK resident for a tax year
- Meet the '90 day test' (see Section 4.6)

Becoming UK resident for a tax year will have major tax consequences, both for income and capital gains. Nonetheless, it may be worthwhile in some cases.

Obviously, it would not be beneficial if any capital gains arose on UK property during the year of UK residence – as these would then be fully exposed to Capital Gains Tax.

The Income Tax position would also need to be taken into account. However, for a non-UK domiciled individual, the costs arising might be acceptable. This is because these individuals only have to pay UK Income Tax on UK source income and on any overseas income which they remit to the UK.

There are additional charges on non-UK domiciled individuals who remain UK resident for seven or more years, but these would not arise in the case of a single year of UK residence.

A non-UK domiciled individual is basically an individual whose permanent home is in another country. For further details, see the Taxcafe.co.uk guide *How to Save Inheritance Tax*.

Example

Salman has been resident and domiciled in Saudi Arabia all his life.

In July 2015, he purchases a house in London for £3m. He uses this as his London home for many years, but never stays in the UK more than 45 days in any tax year.

By early 2025, Salman's house is worth £5m but he is saddened by the fact that he seldom gets to spend much time there. "What the heck" he says to himself and he spends nine months in the house during 2025/26, making him UK resident that year.

By remitting as little of his overseas income arising in that year to the UK as he possibly can, he is able to keep the additional UK Income Tax cost arising to just £20,000. He also avoids making any capital gains on UK assets that year and does not remit the proceeds of any overseas asset disposals to the UK.

Eventually Salman sells the house for £10m in July 2035. His entire £7m gain is subject to Capital Gains Tax but he is able to make a main residence election in favour of the property for the 2025/26 tax year. This enables him to claim principal private residence relief for 2025/26 and for the last eighteen months of his ownership: a total of 2.5 years out of his 20 years of ownership.

Salman's principal private residence relief thus amounts to £875,000 (£7m x 2.5/20), saving him £245,000 in Capital Gains Tax (£875,000 x 28%) – more than ten times his additional Income Tax cost in 2025/26.

A minor additional point is that, if Salman had occasionally rented the property out, he would be able to claim a further £40,000 in private letting relief, saving an additional £11,200 (at 28%).

4.9   MEETING THE '90 DAY TEST'

If becoming UK resident for a year does not appeal to you, the other way to ensure that you are able to make a main residence election in favour of a UK property is to meet the '90 day test' described in Section 4.6.

To do this and yet remain non-resident means paying careful attention to the statutory residence rules in Chapter 6. In particular, it is important to ensure that the 'UK Home Test' set out in Section 6.5 does not apply. This can usually be achieved by ensuring that you also have an overseas home for at least 336 days in the tax year (337 if the year includes a 29th February), and spending more than 30 days there in the same tax year.

Long-Term Non-Residents

Those who have been non-resident for a long time (or have never been UK resident) are in a better position.

Naturally, the 'accommodation tie' will always apply since you have a UK home. But if you have been non-resident for at least the previous three tax years, this single tie will still enable you to spend up to 182 days in the UK without becoming UK resident, so you could easily spend the required 90 days in your UK home.

The following year, you are also likely to have the '90 day tie', but you would still be able to spend up to 120 days in the UK without becoming UK resident. Hence, once again, you could easily spend the required 90 days in your UK home.

You will need to be more careful if you are working in the UK, or have close family in the UK. If **either** the 'family tie' or the 'work tie' applies (but not both) then the 182 days permitted in the first year becomes just 120 days. This would still enable you to spend the required 90 days in your UK home without becoming UK resident. However, it would be very difficult for an unmarried non-resident individual to meet the test again in either of the next two years.

Multiple Tie Strategies

If **both** the 'family tie' and the 'work tie' apply to you then you can only spend a maximum of 90 days in the UK without becoming UK resident. To meet the '90 day test' would thus mean adopting one of the following strategies:

- Spend *exactly* 90 days in your UK home and make sure that you do not spend any other days in the UK in the same tax year (this has to be regarded as a risky strategy – especially when considering the 'Cinderella syndrome' below)

- If you are married, split your time in the UK between you and your spouse, so that neither of you exceeds 90 days but the total time spent in your UK home, between you, is at least 90 days

- Buy a new UK home part way through the tax year so that the '90 day test' is reduced to a level which you can accommodate. For example, if you bought a new UK home on 1st February 2016, you would only need to spend 16 days there in order to be eligible to make a main residence election in favour of the property (covering the period from 1st February to 5th April 2016)

If the 'family tie' and the 'work tie' both continue to apply in the following year then you are very unlikely to be able to meet the '90 day test' without becoming UK resident!

The Benefits

Despite the potential difficulties discussed above, even enabling a property to be elected as a main residence for just one tax year has enormous potential benefits, The same potential savings as we saw for Salman in Section 4.8 are available if you can meet the '90 day test' on a UK property for just one tax year: without the extra Income Tax cost!

For most people with much smaller properties than Salman, the real issue is the practicality of spending 90 days in your UK home and the resultant disruption to your normal life, especially those with their own business or in employment.

Those who are married can at least share this 'burden' with their spouse – perhaps they might be willing to spend a few extra weeks in your UK holiday home to help you out!

The Cinderella Syndrome

It is worth noting that, for the purposes of the '90 day test' you need to be present in your UK home at midnight in order for a day to be counted.

This could mean that, like Cinderella, you may need to leave the ball (or the party, dinner, friend's house, pub, restaurant, etc) early in order to get back home by midnight.

This may seem like a really petty point (indeed it is), but I would not put it past HM Revenue and Customs to make use of it when your day count is exactly 90 or only just over.

4.10 RECENT EMIGRANTS

It is much more difficult for anyone who has only recently become non-resident to meet the '90 day test' whilst remaining non-resident.

Anyone considering emigration (a subject we will look at in Chapter 6) would generally be better off establishing any UK homes as their main residence before they go.

Nonetheless, it is still worth looking at how a recent emigrant might reduce their Capital Gains Tax bill on a UK home.

Anyone who was UK resident in either of the previous two tax years and who has a UK home is likely to have both the 'accommodation tie' and the '90 day tie' and can therefore only spend a maximum of 90 days in the UK without becoming UK resident again.

This means that meeting the '90 day test' for a UK property would necessitate using one of the 'Multiple Tie Strategies' which we looked at in Section 4.9.

In the third tax year as a non-resident, the new emigrant would be able to spend up to 120 days in the UK, so it would then be reasonably easy to meet the '90 day test' on a UK home.

All of this is, however, based on the assumption that none of the other ties set out in Section 6.3 apply. Just one more tie and it would be near impossible for any recent emigrant to meet the '90 day test' in the first two years; and still quite difficult in the third (one of the 'Multiple Tie Strategies' would again be required).

However, despite all this, a married couple who have recently emigrated might sometimes still be able to meet the '90 day test'.

Example

In March 2016, Chris and Sam, a married couple, emigrate to New Zealand where they buy a new home. They do not leave any close family in the UK.

In April 2016, the couple buy a flat in London for £400,000. Initially, they rent the flat out but they also intend to use it as their home when they are visiting the UK.

In April 2017, the tenant moves out and the couple keep the flat available for their own use.

Chris moves into the flat on 20th May 2017 and stays there for 40 days until 29th June. Sam also moves into the flat on 1st June 2017 and stays there for 60 days until 31st July.

Sam makes additional visits to the flat in October 2017 and March 2018: each for 10 days. Sam is working in the UK during these visits and was also working for 14 days during July. However, Sam's days of working in the UK during 2017/18 amount to less than 40 days in total, so the 'work tie' does not apply.

Chris stays in the flat from 20th December 2017 to 5th January 2018, a total of 15 further nights. Both of Chris's visits were purely for personal reasons and no work was carried out.

In total, Chris has spent 55 days in the UK during 2017/18. Sam also spent some time travelling in the UK, which added a further 7 days, so has spent a total of 87 days in the UK during 2017/18. With only two ties applying, both of them have managed to retain their non-resident status for the year.

Between them, however, they have clocked up a total of 107 days in the flat and can thus elect for the property to be treated as their main residence for 2017/18.

The couple continue to use the property as their London residence until January 2019, but they do not manage to meet the '90 day test' for 2018/19.

In February 2019, they resume renting out the flat. They then sell it in October 2020 for £760,000.

The couple are able to claim principal private residence relief for 2017/18 and for their final eighteen months of ownership: a total of 2.5 years out of their total ownership period of 4.5 years (or 54 months). This amounts to £200,000 (sale proceeds, £760,000, less cost, £400,000 = total gain of £360,000 x 2.5/4.5 = £200,000).

The flat was let out for a total of 32 months, but 18 of these are exempt, so the 'gain arising due to the letting' is only 14 months out of a total ownership period of 54 months, i.e. £93,333 (£360,000 x 14/54).

The private letting relief available to the couple is thus the lowest of:

i)   The principal private residence relief: £200,000
ii)   The gain arising due to the letting: £93,333
iii)   £40,000 per person: £80,000

Hence, Chris and Sam can claim private letting relief of £80,000.

Taking both reliefs into account, the chargeable gain on the property is reduced to just £80,000 (£360,000 - £200,000 - £80,000).

After their 2020/21 annual exemptions (estimated at £12,250 each), they might have taxable gains of just £27,750, perhaps giving them Capital Gains Tax bills of as little as £4,995 each (at 18%), or just £9,990 in total.

Note that I have assumed throughout this example that Chris and Sam's New Zealand home remains available to them at all times and that they each spend at least 30 days there in each tax year.

As we can see, by carefully timing their visits to the UK, and their stays in their London flat, the couple were able to remain non-resident and still claim principal private residence relief and private letting relief totalling £280,000. This will have saved them up to £78,400 in Capital Gains Tax (at 28%).

4.11 PERIODS OF ABSENCE

As explained in Section 4.2, where a property qualifies as a main residence at some point during an individual's ownership, certain periods of absence from the property may be included in the principal private residence relief claim. These periods are as follows:

i) Any single period of up to three years, or shorter periods totalling no more than three years, regardless of the reason,

ii) A period of up to four years when the taxpayer or their spouse is required to work elsewhere by reason of their employment or their place of work, and

iii) A period of any length when the taxpayer or their spouse is working in an office or employment whose duties are all performed outside the UK.

However, these temporary absences are only covered by the principal private residence exemption if:

a) Principal private residence relief has not been claimed on any other property in respect of the same period

b) The taxpayer occupies the property as their main residence for a period before the absence period, **and**

c) Either:
   - The taxpayer occupies the property as their main residence for a period after the absence period, or

   - In the case of absences under (ii) or (iii) above, the taxpayer or their spouse is prevented from resuming occupation of the property following their absence by reason of their place of work or a condition imposed by their contract of employment which requires them to reside elsewhere.

A condition imposed on an employee under (c) above needs to be a reasonable condition required to secure the effective performance of the employee's duties.

A Key Change

For disposals taking place prior to 6th April 2015, condition (a) was somewhat different and read as follows:

Neither the taxpayer nor their spouse have any interest in any other property capable of being treated as their main residence under the principal private residence exemption.

In other words, for disposals prior to 6th April 2015, a period of absence could not be included whenever the taxpayer or their spouse owned any other property which was eligible for principal private residence relief.

The new rule applying for disposals taking place after 5th April 2015 is that it is only any period for which the owner actually claims principal private residence relief on another property which must be excluded.

This key change will open a whole new area of tax planning on residential property.

Example

David purchased a property in Darlington in 2001 for use as his main residence. In 2008, he moved to Australia to work full time there. He kept his Darlington property and rented it out.

In 2009, David purchased a property in Australia to use as his main residence there. In early 2016, David gets a good job offer back in the UK and decides to return. He sells his Australian property in March 2016 and returns to the UK on 10th April, where he resumes residence in his Darlington property.

Under the old principal private residence relief rules applying prior to 6th April 2015, David would have been unable to claim relief on his Darlington property for the period from 2009 to March 2016 because he owned another property eligible for relief throughout that period.

Under the new rules, however, David will remain eligible for principal private residence relief on his Darlington property throughout his period of absence because he has not claimed relief on any other property in respect of this period.

If David had sold his Australian property after resuming UK residence, however, he would have lost relief on his Darlington property for the relevant period. This is because, where there is only one private residence for a period, the relief is automatic and not dependent on a claim.

Hence, under these circumstances, David would automatically obtain principal private residence relief (for the period that he resided in his Australian property) on whichever property he sold first.

Naturally, when planning for this sort of situation, David should also take any potential Australian tax liabilities into account.

Final Period of Ownership Exemption

The additional exemption for the last eighteen months of ownership of a qualifying property does not need to be taken into account for the purposes of restricting principal private residence relief on another property.

Example

Let us now suppose that David moved out of his Australian property on 31st March 2016 but did not sell it. Instead, he retained the property and let it out.

He then sold the property eighteen months later, on 30th September 2017 whist UK resident and residing once more in his Darlington property.

David's gain on his Australian property will automatically be fully exempt from Capital Gains Tax as a consequence of principal private residence relief.

However, David will only lose principal private residence relief on his Darlington property for the period that he actually resided in his Australian property as his main residence (2009 to March 2016).

Furthermore, when David sells his Darlington property, he will also be eligible for principal private residence relief for his last eighteen months of ownership of that property: even if this period overlaps with part of the period that he resided in his Australian property.

4.12 PRIVATE RESIDENCES HELD IN TRUST

A trust is a separate legal entity in its own right for tax purposes and here principal private residence relief is no exception. The relief extends to a property held by a trust when the property is the only or main residence of one or more of the trust's beneficiaries.

However, principal private residence relief is not available on a property held by a trust if a hold-over relief claim was made on the transfer of that property into the trust. Similar restrictions apply where a hold over relief claim has been made when a property was transferred out of a trust.

Despite these restrictions, trusts can still be used as a useful mechanism to obtain principal private residence relief on UK properties occupied by adult children or other friends and relatives.

Trusts also have their own annual exemption. This is generally half the amount of an individual's annual exemption (see Section 2.3), but must be further reduced where the same person has transferred assets into more than one trust.

Subject to any available reliefs, trusts pay Capital Gains Tax at the single flat rate of 28%.

4.13 PRIVATE RESIDENCES HELD IN COMPANIES

Companies are not eligible for principal private residence relief or private letting relief.

Furthermore, companies owning UK residential property are subject to the Annual Tax on Enveloped Dwellings and related Capital Gains Tax charges. We will examine these charges in detail in Chapter 5.

Chapter 5

Companies

5.1 WHICH NON-RESIDENT COMPANIES ARE CAUGHT?

In this chapter, we will look at the application of the new Capital Gains Tax charge to non-resident companies and other non-resident corporate entities. For ease of reference, I will refer to all such entities as 'companies' throughout the chapter.

The new charge applies to 'closely held companies'. Broadly speaking, these are companies under the control of five or fewer unconnected individuals. We will take a closer look at the definition of 'closely held companies' in Section 5.2.

Larger institutional investors are exempt from the new Capital Gains Tax charge, including:

- Diversely held companies
- Unit Trusts*
- Open-ended investment companies ('OEICs')*

* - These entities are exempt providing that they meet the 'widely marketed fund' condition.

A diversely help company is a company which is not a 'closely held company': in other words, a company which is not under the control of five or fewer unconnected individuals.

In broad terms, this means that **most non-resident private companies investing in UK residential property will be subject to the new charge**. A company would generally need to be owned by at least 11 unrelated individuals to be exempt: even then, there are additional rules which must be met.

Where a company is exempt from the non-resident Capital Gains Tax charge, it must still report any disposals of UK residential property (as defined in Chapter 3) to HM Revenue and Customs and then claim exemption from the charge.

5.2   CLOSELY HELD COMPANY RULES

A company is a 'closely held company', and thus subject to the non-resident Capital Gains Tax charge, if five or fewer participators control the company.

This is defined as being when five or fewer participators:

i)   Hold, or have the right to acquire, more than 50% of the voting power in the company,

ii)   Possess, or have the right to acquire, interests in the company which would entitle them to more than 50% of the company's assets if the company were wound up, or

iii)   Possess, or have the right to acquire, interests in the company which would entitle them to more than 50% of the company's assets if the company were wound up and the rights of the company's loan creditors were disregarded

Rights and interests under (ii) or (iii) include rights and interests in another company which holds rights or interests in the company under question. For example, if Erica holds 50% of the shares in Company A and it holds 50% of the shares in Company B, then Erica is taken to be entitled to 25% (50% x 50%) of the assets of Company B.

What is a Participator?

A participator is any individual or any legal entity except a:

- Diversely held company (see Section 5.1)
- Unit Trust (meeting the 'widely marketed fund' condition)
- Open-ended investment company (meeting the 'widely marketed fund' condition)
- Qualifying pension scheme
- Person with sovereign immunity from Corporation Tax or Income Tax

A diversely held company is, however, counted as a participator if it is merely acting as a representative, or nominee for another person.

Connected Persons

In determining whether five or fewer participators control a company, any shares or other rights held by an individual's associates must be treated as if they belonged to the individual for this purpose. An individual's associates for this purpose include:

i)   Their spouse
ii) The following relatives:
    o   Mother, father or remoter ancestor
    o   Son, daughter or remoter descendant
    o   Brother or sister

iii) Relatives under (ii) above of the individual's spouse
iv) Spouses of the individual's relatives under (ii) above
vii) Trusts set up the individual, or any of their relatives under (i) to (iv) above

Divided Companies

If a company is structured in such a way that capital gains arising on its assets are wholly or mainly attributable to a division of the company; and if that division would be regarded as close company if it were a separate entity in its own right; then the gains attributable to that division are caught by the non-resident Capital Gains Tax charge.

Anti-Avoidance

Any tax avoidance arrangements designed to prevent a company from being a closely held company are to be disregarded so that the company will be treated as a closely held company for the purpose of the non-resident Capital Gains Tax charge.

5.3   CLOSELY HELD COMPANIES IN PRACTICE

Despite the complexity of the rules set out in Section 5.2, in practice the question of whether most non-resident companies are a 'closely held company' will usually be determined by looking at whether five or fewer unconnected persons hold more than 50% of the company's shares.

Example 1

Eleven unconnected investors set up Merkel Gmbh. The company issues a total of 110 shares: 10 to each investor.

There is no combination of five or fewer individuals that can control the company: any group of five investors holds 45%of the shares.

Merkel Gmbh is therefore a diversely held company and is not subject to the non-resident Capital Gains Tax charge.

Example 1, Part 2

Helmut, one of the investors in Merkel Gmbh, sells his shares to Kurt, one of the other investors. A group of five investors which includes Kurt now holds 55% of the shares.

*As a result of Helmut's share sale, Merkel Gmbh has now become a closely held company and **is** now subject to the non-resident Capital Gains Tax charge.*

Tax Tip

Anyone setting up an investment company like Merkel Gmbh should try to prevent the type of transaction which took place in Part 2 of the example and made the company a closely held company. This can usually be done by way of a shareholders' agreement which prevents such transactions from taking place.

Example 2

A group of 20 investors set up Romanov Inc. The company issues a total of 100 shares: 5 to each investor.

The investors include the following individuals:

- *Nicholas*
- *His wife, Alexandra*
- *Their daughter, Anastasia*
- *Her husband, Boris*

As well as:

- *Anna*
- *Her brother, Yuri*
- *Dimitri, who holds his shares as trustee of a trust set up by Anna for the benefit of her son*

And:

- *Peter*
- *His sister, Catherine*

For the purpose of the closely held company rules, Nicholas is treated as if he holds 20 shares; Anna is treated as if she holds 15; and Peter is treated as if he holds 10.

Combining Nicholas, Anna and Peter's shares with any two other investors brings us to a total of 55 shares: 55% of the company's shares.

Romanov Inc is therefore a closely held company and is subject to the non-resident Capital Gains Tax charge.

As we can see, it is important to know a few things about your fellow investors when you are setting up a non-resident property investment company!

5.4   CALCULATING THE CHARGE

Companies are generally entitled to use any of the three alternative methods set out in Section 3.2 for calculating the chargeable gain arising on a disposal of UK residential property. (Except where the Annual Tax on Enveloped Dwellings applies: see Section 5.5)

Companies are also entitled to claim indexation relief on their chargeable gains and pay tax at Corporation Tax rates, generally 20% (although the charge is still classed as Capital Gains Tax).

Indexation relief is calculated based on the increase in the Retail Prices Index over the relevant period.

Note: All indexation relief rates used in this guide are based on the actual Retail Prices Index statistics for periods up to April 2015 (see Appendix B) and estimated inflation rates of 2.5% per annum thereafter.

The combination of indexation relief and a (generally) lower tax rate means that, although many companies are caught by the charge, the impact is not as severe as for most individuals or trusts.

Example

Clinton Inc owns a UK residential investment property which it purchased for £1m on 5th April 2014. The property is worth £1.05m on 5th April 2015.

The company sells the property on 5th April 2019 for £1.35m.

The gain arising under the main 'default' method is £300,000 (£1.35m – £1.05m), but the company may claim indexation relief for the period from April 2015 to April 2019. This amounts to 10.4%, giving relief of £109,200 (£1.05m x 10.4%) and producing a chargeable gain of £190,800 (£300,000 - £109,200).

The gain arising over the company's entire period of ownership is £350,000 (£1.35m - £1m), but the company may claim indexation relief for the period from April 2014 to April 2019. This amounts to 11.4%, giving relief of £114,000 (£1m x 11.4%) and producing an indexed gain of £236,000 (£350,000 - £114,000). Using the straight line apportionment method then reduces this to a chargeable gain of £188,800 (£236,000 x 4/5).

As we can see, the straight line apportionment method is slightly better in this case, so Clinton Inc elects to use it and pays Capital Gains Tax of £37,760 (£188,800 x 20%).

By way of comparison, let's now look at what would have happened if a non-resident individual, Bill, had owned the same property.

Example, Part 2

Bill's gain under the main 'default' method is simply £300,000 (£1.35m – £1.05m).

The gain arising over his entire period of ownership is £350,000 (£1.35m - £1m). Using the straight line apportionment method then reduces this to a chargeable gain of £280,000 (£350,000 x 4/5).

As we can see, the straight line apportionment method is again better in this case, so Bill elects to use it. His Capital Gains Tax charge will then be somewhere between around £71,810 and £78,400, depending on whether he has used his 2018/19 annual exemption elsewhere and on the level of his UK source income for that year. (And based on an estimated 2018/19 annual exemption of £11,750 and basic rate band of £33,000.)

As we can see, the saving produced by using a company in this case is at least £34,050 (£71,810 - £37,760), possibly as much as £40,640 (£78,400 - £37,760).

5.5   ENVELOPED DWELLINGS

An additional complication for some non-resident companies is that they are also subject to Capital Gains Tax under the Annual Tax on Enveloped Dwellings rules (see Section 5.6).

This charge is often known as 'ATED-related Capital Gains Tax' and applies to any residential dwelling in the UK which is not used for 'business purposes' and which is sold for over £1m (reducing to £500,000 from 6th April 2016).

ATED-related Capital Gains Tax does not apply to individuals or most trusts.

Business use includes renting the property out (to unconnected persons), so most property investment companies will be able to claim exemption from ATED-related Capital Gains Tax, but this charge will apply where property is held for private use.

Where a non-resident company is subject to ATED-related Capital Gains Tax, this charge (which applies at a flat rate of 28% with no indexation relief) takes precedence over the new non-resident Capital Gains Tax charge.

Some property disposals may be subject to both charges: in this case, the company is not able to elect to use the straight line apportionment method, but may elect to have both charges calculated over the entire period of ownership of the property.

Example

Sarkozy S.A., a small French company controlled by Nicolas and his wife, bought four houses in London for £400,000 each on 5th October 2009. All of the houses are initially rented out but Nicolas and his family adopt one as their London residence from 5th October 2015.

Each of the houses is worth £550,000 at 5th April 2015 and £575,000 at 5th April 2016. The company sells the private residence and one of the rented houses for £610,000 each on 5th October 2016.

The Rented Property
The company is subject to non-resident Capital Gains Tax on the rented house for the period from 5th April 2015 to 5th October 2016. The gain over this period is £60,000 (£610,000 - £550,000), but the company may claim indexation relief of £20,900 (£550,000 x 3.8%), leaving a taxable gain of £39,100. The Capital Gains Tax due, at 20% (the Corporation Tax rate), is £7,820.

Alternatively, the company may elect to use the straight line apportionment method. The gain on the property over the whole period of ownership is £210,000 (£610,000 - £400,000), but the company may claim indexation relief of £96,000 (£400,000 x 24.0%), reducing it to £114,000.

Of this, 18 months out of the total ownership period of seven years is subject to Capital Gains Tax, giving a taxable gain of just £24,429 (£114,000 x 1.5/7). The election will therefore be beneficial and will reduce the company's Capital Gains Tax bill to £4,886 (£24,429 x 20%).

The Residence
The property used as a residence is subject to ATED-related Capital Gains Tax on the increase in value from 5th April 2016 to the date of sale. (The start date for this charge is 5th April 2016 because the

property is worth more than £500,000 but not more than £1m.) This charge amounts to £9,800 because the gain of £35,000 (£610,000 - £575,000) is taxed at 28% and no indexation relief is available.

This property is also subject to non-resident Capital Gains Tax at 20% on the £25,000 gain arising over the period from 5th April 2015 to 5th April 2016. This time, the company may claim indexation relief of £13,750 (£550,000 x 2.5%), reducing the gain to £11,250 and producing a Capital Gains Tax bill of £2,250 (£11,250 x 20%).

As things stand, the company will therefore suffer a total Capital Gains Tax bill of £12,050 (£9,800 + £2,250) on this property. However, as an alternative, it may elect to have both charges calculated on the basis of the gain arising over its entire period of ownership.

The company's total gain on the property over seven years amounts to £210,000 (£610,000 - £400,000). The property was in private use for just one year, so the amount of gain subject to ATED-related Capital Gains Tax would be £30,000 (£210,000 x 1/7), giving rise to a Capital Gains Tax bill, at 28%, of £8,400.

The remaining gain of £180,000 would attract indexation relief of £82,286 (£400,000 x 24.0% x 6/7), reducing it to £97,714 and thus giving rise to a Capital Gains Tax bill, at 20%, of £19,543.

Hence, although the election would reduce the ATED-related Capital Gains Tax in this case, it would not be beneficial, as the company's total Capital Gains Tax bill would be increased to £27,943 (£8,400 + £19,543).

5.6   THE ANNUAL TAX ON ENVELOPED DWELLINGS AND RELATED CHARGES

In 2012, the UK Government began to introduce a series of additional tax charges aimed at UK residential property owned by 'non-natural persons'. The definition of 'non-natural persons' includes companies, partnerships where a company is a partner, and collective investment schemes. Most commonly, the charges apply to companies. They do not apply to property investors operating purely as individuals.

These charges apply regardless of where the company or other 'non-natural person' is resident for tax purposes: they apply equally to both UK resident and non-resident companies and other 'non-natural persons'.

Three charges are involved:

- The 15% rate of Stamp Duty Land Tax (see Section 1.7)
- The Annual Tax on Enveloped Dwellings
- Capital Gains Tax at 28% on the disposal of the property (also known as 'ATED-related Capital Gains Tax')

However, the charges only apply to single dwellings worth in excess of the specified threshold. They do not apply by reference to the total value of the property portfolio.

Business Exemption

The good news for most property investors operating through a company (or any other 'non-natural person') is that properties are exempt from these charges if they are being used in a business: including a property rental business. Hence, in most cases, property investment companies should be exempt from the three charges; although it is essential to ensure that properties are being acquired for use in the business, and continue to be held for business purposes thereafter.

The bad news, however, is that any company or other 'non-natural person' which is eligible for this exemption will need to claim it – whenever they buy property worth more than £500,000 for Stamp Duty Land Tax purposes; and on an annual basis when they own property worth more than the specified threshold for the purposes of the Annual Tax on Enveloped Dwellings.

Hence, even if there is no extra tax, there will still be plenty of extra administration to deal with!

Falling Thresholds

Prior to 20th March 2014, the three charges described above only applied to property worth in excess of £2m. However, the 2014 Budget included the announcement that the scope of these charges was to be substantially increased over the next couple of years, so that they will eventually apply to property worth in excess of just £500,000.

The 15% Stamp Duty Land Tax charge was applied to purchases of relevant property for a price in excess of £500,000 with effect from 20th March 2014.

The thresholds for the Annual Tax on Enveloped Dwellings and Capital Gains Tax charges are being reduced progressively, as detailed below.

The Annual Tax on Enveloped Dwellings

The Annual Tax on Enveloped Dwellings has applied to property worth in excess of £2m since 1st April 2013. It has applied to property worth in excess of £1m, but not more than £2m, since 1st April 2015.

The rates applying for 2015/16 are:

Property Value	Charge
Over £1m, but not more than £2m	£7,000
Over £2m, but not more than £5m	£23,350
Over £5m, but not more than £10m	£54,450
Over £10m, but not more than £20m	£109,050
Over £20m	£218,200

The Annual Tax on Enveloped Dwellings will apply to property worth over £500,000, but no more than £1m, from 1st April 2016 and will initially be charged at £3,500 per annum on these properties.

All of the Annual Tax on Enveloped Dwellings charges will be increased annually in line with the Consumer Prices Index.

ATED-related Capital Gains Tax

The 28% Capital Gains Tax charge applies to gains on properties worth over £2m accruing after 5th April 2013.

It applies to gains on properties worth over £1m, but no more than £2m, accruing after 5th April 2015.

It will apply to gains on properties worth over £500,000, but no more than £1m, accruing after 5th April 2016.

In each case, the ATED-related Capital Gains Tax charge only applies to the increase in the property's value between the specified date and the date of disposal.

Non-resident companies which are caught by this charge on a property sold for more than £500,000, but not more than £1m, will also still need to pay non-resident Capital Gains Tax on the gain arising between 5th April 2015 and 5th April 2016.

Example

On 5th April 2015, Chancellor Investments Ltd, a company based in Jersey, bought two properties in London for £750,000 each: numbers 10 and 11 Dingnow Street.

No. 10 Dingnow Street is used as a rental property and is rented out to unconnected tenants.

No. 11 Dingnow Street is used as a private residence by George, the company's owner.

Both properties are sold on 5th April 2019 at a price of £1m each.

The Stamp Duty Land Tax arising on the purchase of No. 10 (the rental property) amounted to £27,500 at normal rates. Chancellor Investments Ltd will be subject to non-resident Capital Gains Tax on the gain arising on the sale of this property: £222,500 (£1m - £750,000 - £27,500). The company may, however, claim indexation relief (see Section 5.4). This amounts to 10.4%, giving relief of £80,860 (£777,500 x 10.4%).

The company thus pays Capital Gains Tax at 20% on £141,640 (£222,500 - £80,860), which is just £28,328.

This property will be exempt from the Annual Tax on Enveloped Dwellings, but the company will have to claim exemption from the charge on annual returns for 2016/17, 2017/18 and 2018/19.

The Stamp Duty Land Tax arising on the purchase of No. 11 (the private residence) will be at 15%: i.e. £112,500.

The company will also be subject to the Annual Tax on Enveloped Dwellings at £3,500 for 2016/17, 2017/18 and 2018/19. (It will actually be slightly more in 2017/18 and 2018/19 but we will ignore these increases for the sake of illustration.)

When the company sells the property, it will be subject to non-resident Capital Gains Tax on the part of the gain arising up to 5th April 2016. Let's say the property was worth £875,000 at that date, so this part of the gain amounts to £12,500 (£875,000 - £750,000 - £112,500).

Indexation relief for this period, at 2.5%, amounts to £21,563 (£862,500 x 2.5%). This exceeds the amount of the gain, so no Capital Gains Tax is due. This may sound like a good outcome, but it only happens because of the huge amount of Stamp Duty Land Tax paid on the purchase of the property. Furthermore, the company is unable to claim any loss in respect of the excess indexation relief.

The remaining £125,000 of the gain on this property (i.e. the part of the gain arising between 6th April 2016 and 5th April 2019) is subject to Capital Gains Tax at a flat rate of 28%, i.e. £35,000.

In total, the tax paid on the private residence amounts to £158,000 (£112,500 + £3,500 x 3 + £35,000), compared with just £55,828 (£27,500 + £28,328) on the rental property. George might also be subject to Income Tax charges in respect of his private use of No. 11. If so, the company would be subject to Class 1A National Insurance on this too.

Similarly, where any other UK residential property is only caught by the ATED-related Capital Gains Tax charge for part of a non-resident company's period of ownership falling after 5th April 2015, the company will again need to pay non-resident Capital Gains Tax on the part of the gain arising after that date which is not subject to ATED-related Capital Gains Tax.

See Section 5.5 for another example of the interaction between ATED-related Capital Gains Tax and non-resident Capital Gains Tax on the same property.

In short, what both examples tell us is that holding private residences through a company has become a very expensive business!

Chapter 6

A Guide to Emigration and Residence

6.1 INTRODUCTION TO EMIGRATION

As we know, non-residents are subject to Capital Gains Tax on the disposal of UK residential property after 5th April 2015.

Nonetheless, it is important to remember that:

- Non-resident Capital Gains Tax only applies to UK residential property
- Only the increase in the property's value after 5th April 2015 is subject to Capital Gains Tax

The implications of these points are explored further in Chapter 7.

In this chapter, we will concentrate on the issue of achieving non-UK residence in the first place!

6.2 THE BENEFITS OF EMIGRATION

UK investors facing substantial Capital Gains Tax liabilities sometimes avoid some or all of those liabilities by emigrating.

However, merely going on a world cruise for a year will not be sufficient, as it is necessary to become non-resident for more than five years in order to avoid any UK Capital Gains Tax.

This is a complex field of tax planning, which really requires a separate guide in its own right. Furthermore, matters have been further complicated by the introduction of the statutory residence test, which applies from 2013/14 onwards. In this section, I am therefore only going to give you a flavour of what is involved: there are many other factors and considerations to be taken into account which I simply do not have space to cover here.

Nonetheless, the main points worth noting are:

- Emigration must generally be permanent, or at least long-term (a period of more than five years is required for those emigrating after 5th April 2013; a period of at least five complete UK tax years is required for those who emigrated earlier).

- Disposals should be deferred until non-residence has been achieved.

- Limited return visits to the UK are permitted (see Section 6.3).

- Resuming UK residence (under the statutory residence rules) before the expiry of the required period discussed above may result in substantial Capital Gains Tax liabilities.

- It is essential to ensure that there is no risk of inadvertently becoming liable for some form of capital taxation elsewhere. (There is no point in 'jumping out of the frying pan and into the fire!')

Emigration to avoid UK tax is a strategy which is generally only worth contemplating when the stakes are high. Naturally, therefore, detailed professional advice is always essential.

The following example illustrates the broad outline of what is involved.

Example

Eleanor has been a highly successful UK property investor for many years. By early 2015, she has potential Capital Gains Tax liabilities on her UK investment property portfolio of over £2,000,000.

She therefore decides to emigrate and, on 3rd April 2015, she flies to Utopia where she settles down to a new life.

During the 2015/16 tax year, Eleanor sells all her UK properties, but is mostly exempt from Capital Gains Tax as a non-resident. Her only exposure to Capital Gains Tax arises from any increases in the value of her UK residential property between 5th April 2015 and the date of disposal of the properties.

Eventually, however, Eleanor decides that she wants to return home and, on 8th April 2020, she comes back to the UK to live.

As Eleanor was non-resident for over five years, she will remain exempt from Capital Gains Tax on the remaining, more substantial, part of her capital gains.

Notes to the Example

i)   Utopia does not exist. Real countries have their own tax systems and may potentially tax immigrants like Eleanor on their UK capital gains. It is therefore always essential to take detailed local professional advice in the destination country.

ii)   The sales giving rise to capital gains must be deferred until after non-residence has been achieved. From 2013/14 onwards, 'split year' treatment is available, meaning that, under certain circumstances, the emigrant may effectively be regarded as non-resident from the day after the date of departure. Nonetheless, the position will often be uncertain and it will therefore generally be wiser to defer sales until the tax year after the year of departure (e.g. until at least 6th April 2015 in Eleanor's case).

iii)   If Eleanor had returned to the UK to live within five years or less, all of her property disposals in 2015/16 would have become fully liable to Capital Gains Tax. The gains would then be treated as if they had arisen in the tax year in which Eleanor returned to the UK (apart from the small element already taxed during 2015/16). To avoid this, the emigrant must remain non-resident for at least five years and a day. My suggestion would thus be to ensure that there is a clear period of at least five years and a day between the date of departure and the date of return (e.g. Eleanor should not return until at least 5th April 2020: five years and two days after her date of departure) – but see also points (iv) and (v) below.

iv)   For those emigrating after 5th April 2013, 'split year' treatment is again available on their return to the UK in order to determine if they have achieved the requisite period of non-residence. However, achieving 'split year' treatment requires the taxpayer to adhere to certain circumstances as prescribed by a highly complex set of rules so the position will often remain uncertain. For this reason, I would generally suggest that it is safer to remain non-resident until after the end of the tax year in which the fifth anniversary of the day after the date of departure falls (e.g. until at least 6th April 2020 in Eleanor's case).

v)   As explained above, those who emigrated before 6th April 2013 must remain non-resident for at least five complete tax years and cannot use 'split year' treatment to determine whether their period of non-UK residence has been sufficiently long. The question of whether such emigrants have retained their non-UK residence in 2013/14 and later years will be determined using the new statutory residence test.

For the purpose of point (ii) above, it is important to bear in mind that the date of disposal for Capital Gains Tax purposes is the date of contract (or the date that a contract becomes unconditional), not the date of completion.

6.3   VISITS TO THE UK

To remain non-resident, an individual must limit their visits to the UK. For 2013/14 onwards, the maximum amount of visits to the UK is based on a highly complex set of rules included within the new statutory residence test.

Set out below is a guide to the maximum amount of visits which an individual can usually make to the UK without losing their non-resident status.

The first step is to consider whether an individual meets one of the automatic tests for UK residence or non-residence. These tests are applied in a prescribed order. If one of these tests is met, the position is automatically determined and no other tests are required.

Automatic Residence/Non-Residence

Firstly, any individual who spends more than 182 days in the UK in a tax year is automatically UK resident for that year.

Secondly, an individual is regarded as automatically **non-resident** if:

- They spend less than 16 days in the UK in the tax year,

- They spend less than 46 days in the UK in the tax year and were non-resident in each of the previous three tax years, or

- They work full-time overseas over the tax year, with no significant breaks from their overseas work

The 'working full-time overseas test' is highly complex; so detailed professional advice is essential if you are aiming to rely on it!

Thirdly, an individual is regarded as automatically **UK resident** if:

- They maintain a UK home in the year but no overseas home (this, again, is quite a complex test: see Section 6.5 for further details), or

- They work full-time in the UK for a period of at least 365 days, any part of which (even just one day) falls during the tax year. Full-time is generally taken to mean more than 3 hours per day.

Ties

If none of the automatic tests apply, the maximum number of days which a non-resident may spend in the UK is determined by the number of 'ties' which they have with the UK. The 'ties' taken into account for this purpose are:

i)   The Family Tie

The individual has a spouse, common-law partner, or minor child who is resident in the UK. A minor child need only be counted if the individual sees them on more than 60 days in the tax year. Separated spouses do not need to be counted.

ii) The Accommodation Tie

The individual has a home or other accommodation available to them in the UK for at least 91 consecutive days during the tax year and spends at least one night there during the tax year (or spends at least 16 nights there during the tax year if the available accommodation is the home of a close relative).

iii) The Work Tie

The individual works in the UK for more than three hours on at least 40 days during the tax year.

iv) The 90-Day Tie

The individual spent more than 90 days in the UK in either of the two previous tax years.

v) The Country Tie

There is no other country where the individual was present at midnight on more days during the tax year than in the UK.

Maximum Visits

The maximum permitted visits to the UK also depend on whether the individual was UK resident in any of the three previous tax years, as follows:

Maximum Visits If UK Resident in One or More of the Previous Three Years

No. of Ties	Maximum Visits
0	182 Days
1	120 Days
2	90 Days
3	45 Days
4 or 5	15 Days

Maximum Visits If Not UK Resident in Any of the Previous Three Years

No. of Ties	Maximum Visits
0 or 1	182 Days
2	120 Days
3	90 Days
4	45 Days

(The 'country tie' is disregarded in this case.)

Practical Implications

Every individual will face a different set of circumstances, so it is difficult to provide definitive advice which works in every case.

Generally, however, an individual can always achieve non-residence by limiting return visits to the UK to 15 days or less for the first three tax years after departure and to 45 days or less per year thereafter.

Typically, a UK property investor seeking to avoid Capital Gains Tax by emigrating will usually be able to avoid the 'work tie' and the 'country tie' but will often be subject to the 'accommodation tie', especially if they still have any family in the UK. The '90-day tie' will also generally be unavoidable for the first two years after departure. Whether the 'family tie' applies will depend very much on personal circumstances.

Hence, we can generally expect most property investors to have two or three 'ties' in the first two years after departure, meaning that return visits would need to be limited to a maximum of either 45 or 90 days in each tax year.

From the third year onwards, this 'typical' investor would then have only one or two ties and could return for longer periods but anything over 90 days would create a new 'tie' once again, so should probably be avoided.

In short, most property investors seeking to avoid Capital Gains Tax through emigration should probably limit return visits to a maximum of 90 days in each tax year, and no more than 45 days in each of the first two tax years after departure where they have a spouse, partner or minor child in the UK.

In some cases, however, return visits will need to be limited to no more than 15 days per tax year for the first three years and no more than 45 days per tax year thereafter: especially where the 'work tie' may apply.

Longer visits will be possible in some cases but detailed professional advice is essential!

Retaining a UK Home

Retaining a home in the UK may alter the position dramatically. Unless one of the automatic non-residence tests set out above applies, it will be essential to ensure that the 'UK Home Test' set out in Section 6.5 does not apply.

The 'UK Home Test' is, however, easily avoided by ensuring that you also have an overseas home for at least 336 days in the tax year (337 if the year includes 29th February), and spend more than 30 days there in the same tax year.

Even then, the 'accommodation tie' will generally apply.

Nonetheless, despite these drawbacks, there are potential savings to be made on a UK home. See Sections 4.9 and 4.10 for a more detailed analysis.

Earlier Years

For 2012/13 and earlier years, the general rules on return visits were:

- They could not exceed 182 days in any one tax year
- They had to average less than 91 days per year

However, this was only one aspect of the situation and must be regarded as the minimum criterion for maintaining non-resident status. In practice, HM Revenue and Customs looked at many other factors and the more links that the individual maintained with the UK, the more likely they were to continue to be UK resident, and hence still liable for UK Capital Gains Tax.

6.4 WHICH DAYS MUST BE COUNTED IN A VISIT?

The general rule is that any day on which you are present in the UK at midnight is counted for the purpose of the tests in Section 6.3. In other words, we actually count nights rather than days!

This is subject to exclusions for:

- Days of arrival, when you are merely in transit from one foreign country to another, you leave the UK the next day, and do not carry out any other activities while in the UK.

- Days when you are prevented from leaving the UK due to exceptional circumstances beyond your control (up to a maximum of 60 such days in a tax year).

From 2013/14 onwards, any individual who has been UK resident in any of the previous three tax years and who has three or more 'ties' (see Section 6.3) must also count any other days when they are present in the UK at **any time** – subject to an exclusion for the first 30 such days. (These days count as part of the individual's visits to the UK but do not count towards the '90-day tie'.)

6.5 THE UK HOME TEST

Unless one of the automatic non-residence tests set out in Section 6.3 applies, any individual who meets the 'UK Home Test' for a tax year will automatically be treated as UK resident for that tax year. The 'UK Home Test' is as follows:

i)   There is a period of 91 or more consecutive days, of which at least 30 days fall into the tax year, during which the individual has a home in the UK,

ii) In that same period, the individual either has:

- No home overseas, or
- No home overseas in which the individual is present on **more than** 30 days during the tax year,

iii) And the individual is present in their UK home on at least 30 days in the tax year.

Note that it is days on which the individual is physically present in the home at any time (not just at midnight) which are counted for the purposes of parts (ii) and (iii) of this test.

Avoiding the test is easily achieved by having an overseas home available for at least 336 days in the tax year (337 if the year includes 29th February), and spending at least 30 days there in the same tax year.

However, it is essential to remember that an overseas property can only be counted as a home when it is **available** to the individual!

Wealth Warning

Renting out your overseas property will mean that it is no longer your home. Renting it out for more than 90 days could therefore mean that you meet the 'UK Home Test' and automatically become UK resident.

6.6   YEAR OF DEATH

The rules set out in Section 6.3 do not apply in the year of death, when special rules apply instead.

Chapter 7

Tax Saving Tips

7.1 INTRODUCTION

The non-resident Capital Gains Tax charge only applies to gains on UK residential property arising after 5th April 2015.

This leaves plenty of scope for current non-residents and those intending to emigrate in the future to save tax through careful planning.

7.2 EXISTING GAINS

For those UK investors with large existing capital gains in their portfolio, emigration remains a good way to avoid Capital Gains Tax.

Example

Yvonne has a large portfolio of UK residential property. At 5th April 2015, the total gains on her portfolio amounted to around £2m. Selling her portfolio whilst still a UK resident would give her a Capital Gains Tax bill of up to £560,000.

Instead, Yvonne emigrates, becoming non-resident for tax purposes. She sells her portfolio a short time later, when her total gains amount to £2,150,000.

Yvonne is only subject to Capital Gains Tax on the £150,000 of additional gains arising after 5th April 2015. After deducting her 2015/16 annual exemption of £11,100, she has taxable gains of £138,900, giving her a maximum tax bill of just £38,892 – not bad for a portfolio with over £2m of gains in it!

See Chapter 6 for a detailed examination of some of the crucial points to bear in mind when considering emigrating for tax purposes.

7.3 FUTURE GAINS

The non-resident Capital Gains Tax charge will reduce the effectiveness of emigration as a Capital Gains Tax planning strategy in the future, but those with large existing gains, like Yvonne in Section 7.2, could still benefit.

In our example in Section 7.2, Yvonne sold her portfolio fairly soon after April 2015, so her tax bill was not too large. Let us now suppose instead, however, that she waits several years and eventually sells her portfolio at a total gain of £3m. Her Capital Gains Tax bill would now be 28% of the £1m gain arising after 5th April 2015 – a total of £280,000 (ignoring her annual exemption). Is there anything she could have done to reduce this burden?

To begin with, there are simple steps which Yvonne could take, like selling one property in each tax year to maximise the savings produced by her annual exemptions and basic rate band.

Selling a property in a tax year when the annual exemption is fully available (i.e. when the individual has no other chargeable gains in the same year) will produce a saving of up to £3,108 (£11,100 x 28% - using 2015/16 rates).

Selling a property in a tax year when the individual has no UK source income, or has UK source income of less than any available personal allowance (see Section 2.2), could produce further savings of up to £3,179 (£31,785 x 10% - again using 2015/16 rates; 10% being the difference between the higher Capital Gains Tax rate of 28% and the lower Capital Gains Tax rate of 18%).

Yvonne might not be able to achieve all of these savings (her UK source income probably exceeds her personal allowance), but another non-resident individual who times their UK residential property sales carefully could save up to £6,287 on each sale (£3,108 + £3,179 – sticking to 2015/16 rates once more).

Another simple step is to put UK residential properties into joint names with a spouse in order to enable the non-resident couple to benefit from two annual exemptions and basic rate bands.

Wealth Warning

Transfers between spouses are generally exempt from Capital Gains Tax but care needs to be taken where one is UK resident and the other is not, as immediate Capital Gains Tax charges can sometimes arise under these circumstances.

7.4 VALUATIONS

Another simple step being considered by many property investors who are already non-resident, or who are considering emigration in the future, is to have their UK residential property portfolio valued at 5th April 2015.

A good robust valuation carried out now may be extremely useful in the future when the issue of the property's value at that date becomes critical. By obtaining professional valuations near to the relevant time, they will carry more weight in the future and are less likely to be challenged.

In Yvonne's case, in Section 7.2, we saw that her portfolio had gains of 'around £2m' at 5th April 2015. If valuations as at that date are only carried out several years later, this rough figure may well prevail. If, instead, she has the valuations carried out now, whilst we are still fairly near to 5th April 2015, she might find these indicate that the existing gains at that date are actually greater. Every additional £10,000 of value at 5th April 2015 indicated by her valuations will eventually save her £2,800 in UK Capital Gains Tax.

Having your properties valued at 5th April 2015 will give you a better idea of your Capital Gains Tax exposure in the future when considering whether, or when, to sell your properties. It is hard to do any tax planning without having some idea of the tax at stake!

Valuations will also enable you to assess whether you are better off calculating your gains under the main 'default' method, or using straight line apportionment. It is only by being able to compare the results of both methods that you will be able to achieve the best outcome.

Furthermore, as explained in Section 4.5, by not having a valuation at 5th April 2015, you could be denied double tax relief in your country of residence for some of the Capital Gains Tax you pay in the UK.

Having your entire portfolio valued at one time may turn out a lot cheaper than having each property valued piecemeal as you sell them.

Finally, it is worth bearing in mind that the cost of having a property valued for the purpose of a Capital Gains Tax calculation is itself deductible from the capital gain arising.

7.5 CHANGE YOUR PORTFOLIO

It is worth bearing in mind that non-resident Capital Gains Tax charges only apply to UK residential property.

Hence, an investor might benefit by selling off their UK residential property portfolio and reinvesting the proceeds in either:

a) Overseas property, or
b) Commercial property in the UK

Naturally, an investor who is currently UK resident should wait until they are non-resident before beginning this process: unless they have some properties which they can sell with little or no Capital Gains Tax liability at the moment (e.g. a property with a small gain which is covered by their annual exemption).

Those who are already non-resident may benefit by starting a similar process now, with a view to disposing of all UK residential property as soon as possible, whilst the gains arising after 5th April 2015 are still fairly small.

7.6 USING A COMPANY

Another potential strategy may be to transfer UK residential properties into a company: as soon as possible for those who are already non-resident; or shortly after emigration for those who are currently still UK resident.

The transfer will give rise to some Capital Gains Tax, but this will only be on the increase in value after 5th April 2015.

Future gains after the transfer will not completely escape Capital Gains Tax but, as we saw in Section 5.4, holding the properties in a company could reduce the amount of tax payable quite significantly.

Properties worth over £500,000 which are not being rented out as part of a property rental business should generally be excluded from such a transfer, however, due to the charges described in Section 5.6.

7.7 FURNISHED HOLIDAY LETS

Gains of up to £10m which an individual realises on the disposal of a qualifying trading business are eligible for entrepreneurs' relief. This reduces the Capital Gains Tax rate applying to just 10%.

Furnished holiday lettings are deemed to be a qualifying trading business for the purpose of entrepreneurs' relief.

To obtain entrepreneurs' relief, the owner must either dispose of the whole business (not just individual properties) or cease the business (or allow it to cease to qualify as a furnished holiday letting business) and then sell the properties within three years thereafter.

The really interesting point is that a property only needs to qualify as a furnished holiday let for one year in order for the owner to be eligible for entrepreneurs' relief.

A non-resident individual who is able to convert their UK residential property into furnished holiday lettings for a year or more before selling those properties could save up to £1.8m. The potential savings for a couple are up to £3.6m.

There are detailed rules which determine whether a property qualifies as a furnished holiday let. These, together with more details on entrepreneurs' relief, are included in the Taxcafe.co.uk guide *How to Save Property Tax*.

7.8 FURTHER CONSIDERATIONS

Many of the strategies described in this chapter have additional tax implications, and it is also essential to consider the overseas tax implications arising in the investor's country of residence, nationality, and the country where properties are located. Hence, professional advice is essential!

Nonetheless, some careful planning should enable many property investors to significantly reduce the impact of the non-resident Capital Gains Tax charge.

Appendix A

UK Tax Rates and Allowances: 2014/15 to 2016/17

	Rates	2014/15 £	2015/16 £	2016/17 £
Income Tax				
Personal allowance		10,000	10,600	10,800
Basic rate band	20%	31,865	31,785	31,900
Higher rate/Threshold	40%	41,865	42,385	42,700
Personal allowance withdrawal				
Effective rate/From	60%	100,000	100,000	100,000
To		120,000	121,200	121,600
Super tax rate/Threshold	45%	150,000	150,000	150,000
Starting rate band (2)	0%	2,880	5,000	5,000
Marriage allowance (3)		n/a	1,060	1,080
Personal savings allowance		n/a	n/a	1,000(4)
National Insurance				
Primary threshold	9%/12%	7,956	8,060	8,110(1)
Upper earnings limit	2%	41,865	42,385	42,700
Secondary threshold	13.8%	7,956	8,112	8,216(1)
Employment allowance		2,000	2,000	2,000
Class 2 – per week		2.75	2.80	2.85(1)
Small earnings exception		5,885	5,965	5,995(1)
Pension Contributions				
Annual allowance		40,000	40,000	40,000
Lifetime allowance		1.25m	1.25m	1m
Capital Gains Tax				
Annual exemption		11,000	11,100	11,200(1)
Entrepreneurs' relief				
Rate/Lifetime limit	10%	10m	10m	10m
Inheritance Tax				
Nil Rate Band		325,000	325,000	325,000
Annual Exemption		3,000	3,000	3,000

Notes
1. Estimated, based on RPI/CPI inflation at 1.0%/0.5% respectively
2. Applies to interest and other savings income only. 10% rate applies in 2014/15
3. Available to married couples where neither pays higher rate tax
4. £500 for higher rate taxpayers; not available to 'super tax' payers

Retail Prices Index

	1982	1983	1984	1985	1986	1987	1988	1989
Jan		82.61	86.84	91.20	96.25	100.0	103.3	111.0
Feb		82.97	87.20	91.94	96.60	100.4	103.7	111.8
Mar	79.44	83.12	87.48	92.80	96.73	100.6	104.1	112.3
Apr	81.04	84.28	88.64	94.78	97.67	101.8	105.8	114.3
May	81.62	84.64	88.97	95.21	97.85	101.9	106.2	115.0
Jun	81.85	84.84	89.20	95.41	97.79	101.9	106.6	115.4
Jul	81.88	85.30	89.10	95.23	97.52	101.8	106.7	115.5
Aug	81.90	85.68	89.94	95.49	97.82	102.1	107.9	115.8
Sep	81.85	86.06	90.11	95.44	98.30	102.4	108.4	116.6
Oct	82.26	86.36	90.67	95.59	98.45	102.9	109.5	117.5
Nov	82.66	86.67	90.95	95.92	99.29	103.4	110.0	118.5
Dec	82.51	86.89	90.87	96.05	99.62	103.3	110.3	118.8

	1990	1991	1992	1993	1994	1995	1996	1997
Jan	119.5	130.2	135.6	137.9	141.3	146.0	150.2	154.4
Feb	120.2	130.9	136.3	138.8	142.1	146.9	150.9	155.0
Mar	121.4	131.4	136.7	139.3	142.5	147.5	151.5	155.4
Apr	125.1	133.1	138.8	140.6	144.2	149.0	152.6	156.3
May	126.2	133.5	139.3	141.1	144.7	149.6	152.9	156.9
Jun	126.7	134.1	139.3	141.0	144.7	149.8	153.0	157.5
Jul	126.8	133.8	138.8	140.7	144.0	149.1	152.4	157.5
Aug	128.1	134.1	138.9	141.3	144.7	149.9	153.1	158.5
Sep	129.3	134.6	139.4	141.9	145.0	150.6	153.8	159.3
Oct	130.3	135.1	139.9	141.8	145.2	149.8	153.8	159.5
Nov	130.0	135.6	139.7	141.6	145.3	149.8	153.9	159.6
Dec	129.9	135.7	139.2	141.9	146.0	150.7	154.4	160.0

	1998	1999	2000	2001	2002	2003	2004	2005
Jan	159.5	163.4	166.6	171.1	173.3	178.4	183.1	188.9
Feb	160.3	163.7	167.5	172.0	173.8	179.3	183.8	189.6
Mar	160.8	164.1	168.4	172.2	174.5	179.9	184.6	190.5
Apr	162.6	165.2	170.1	173.1	175.7	181.2	185.7	191.6
May	163.5	165.6	170.7	174.2	176.2	181.5	186.5	192.0
Jun	163.4	165.6	171.1	174.4	176.2	181.3	186.8	192.2
Jul	163.0	165.1	170.5	173.3	175.9	181.3	186.8	192.2
Aug	163.7	165.5	170.5	174.0	176.4	181.6	187.4	192.6
Sep	164.4	166.2	171.7	174.6	177.6	182.5	188.1	193.1
Oct	164.5	166.5	171.6	174.3	177.9	182.6	188.6	193.3
Nov	164.4	166.7	172.1	173.6	178.2	182.7	189.0	193.6
Dec	164.4	167.3	172.2	173.4	178.5	183.5	189.9	194.1

	2006	2007	2008	2009	2010	2011	2012	2013
Jan	193.4	201.6	209.8	210.1	217.9	229.0	238.0	245.8
Feb	194.2	203.1	211.4	211.4	219.2	231.3	239.9	247.6
Mar	195.0	204.4	212.1	211.3	220.7	232.5	240.8	248.7
Apr	196.5	205.4	214.0	211.5	222.8	234.4	242.5	249.5
May	197.7	206.2	215.1	212.8	223.6	235.2	242.4	250.0
Jun	198.5	207.3	216.8	213.4	224.1	235.2	241.8	249.7
Jul	198.5	206.1	216.5	213.4	223.6	234.7	242.1	249.7
Aug	199.2	207.3	217.2	214.4	224.5	236.1	243.0	251.0
Sep	200.1	208.0	218.4	215.3	225.3	237.9	244.2	251.9
Oct	200.4	208.9	217.7	216.0	225.8	238.0	245.6	251.9
Nov	201.1	209.7	216.0	216.6	226.8	238.5	245.6	252.1
Dec	202.7	210.9	212.9	218.0	228.4	239.4	246.8	253.4

	2014	2015
Jan	252.6	255.4
Feb	254.2	256.7
Mar	254.8	257.1
Apr	255.7	258.0
May	255.9	
Jun	256.3	
Jul	256.0	
Aug	257.0	
Sep	257.6	
Oct	257.7	
Nov	257.1	
Dec	257.5	

The European Union &
The European Economic Area

The European Union

The 28 member states of the European Union are:

Austria	admitted 1 January 1995
Belgium	founding member
Bulgaria	admitted 1 January 2007
Croatia	admitted 1 July 2013
Cyprus	admitted 1 May 2004
Czech Republic	admitted 1 May 2004
Denmark	admitted 1 January 1973
Estonia	admitted 1 May 2004
Finland	admitted 1 January 1995
France	founding member
Germany	founding member
Greece	admitted 1 January 1981
Hungary	admitted 1 May 2004
Irish Republic	admitted 1 January 1973
Italy	founding member
Latvia	admitted 1 May 2004
Lithuania	admitted 1 May 2004
Luxembourg	founding member
Malta	admitted 1 May 2004
Netherlands	founding member
Poland	admitted 1 May 2004
Portugal	admitted 1 January 1986
Romania	admitted 1 January 2007
Slovakia	admitted 1 May 2004
Slovenia	admitted 1 May 2004
Spain	admitted 1 January 1986
Sweden	admitted 1 January 1995
United Kingdom	admitted 1 January 1973

The European Economic Area comprises the 28 member states of the European Union plus Iceland, Liechtenstein and Norway.